The

Business

of

Blessing

The Biblical Blueprint for a God-Abundant Business

SARAH-JANE ETHAN

For the accompanying 'Business of Blessing - Study Guide',
including 12 page Business Plan template, visit:
www.businessofblessing.com

What Others are Saying:

"WARNING! THIS BOOK MAY CHANGE YOUR LIFE"

"The first chapter literally blew me away.
I was really impacted by the concept of God seeking the maximum reward for the investment that he has put in us. I could feel my faith rising as this truth went in. I have actually made some huge decisions since reading this book, and the wisdom and faith I got from Sarah-Jane was definitely integral to making these changes. SJ's effervescence, enthusiasm, faith and integrity all come through in the book, which is one of the reasons that it is so easy to read. She seems to challenge you with a smile on her face, whilst always drawing you back to God and His word."

— Lindy Rogers, photographer

"CONTAGIOUS"

The Business of Blessing is a faith-expanding challenge to soar beyond the mediocre and secure. Sarah-Jane's grasp of purposeful stewardship— leaving fear behind to see how the Lord can use your business to add value and blessing to others— is contagious. She combines time-proven business principles with her knowledge of scripture, and a good dose of anecdotal encouragement, to spark a reckless abandonment to Christ in the hearts of her readers."

— Brad Smith, business owner of 35 years

"A MUST-READ"

This book is a must-read for all budding entrepreneurs and those already established in business. It will challenge anyone who is stuck in their comfort zone waiting for a miracle. Sarah-Jane comes from a place of wisdom and experience and there are so many nuggets of wisdom throughout the book. She is honest and transparent. You can tell that she just wants everyone to experience the same success she has and live life to their highest God-given potential.

— Fiona NG, lifestyle blogger and e-commerce entrepreneur

2

"I HONESTLY BELIEVE THAT, THROUGH THIS BOOK, GOD CAN DO SOMETHING INCREDIBLE IN THE LIFE OF OUR CHURCH"

I loved Sarah-Jane's challenge to step out without fear.
It wasn't a gentle suggestion, it was a full blown '*I dare you*' which shows her faith in an unfailing God. What if we all dared to step out, live generously and fearlessly in the name of Jesus?
Who knows what would happen!
SJ's faith filled testimony, poured out on paper, is beyond encouraging and truly inspiring. I absolutely loved it!

- Katie Etherton, family business owner

"CAN'T PUT IT DOWN"

This book is kicking my butt! I can't put it down!
Sarah-Jane has a real gift for writing, inspiring and stirring passion and Godly confidence in others. I had little motivation in my business but this book has inspired and challenged me. It is a brilliant balance of biblical challenge, encouragement and practical advice. As soon as I started reading it, I couldn't put it down, I just wanted to soak it all up as much as I could.
SJ is honest, refreshing and very relatable. I have a refreshed perspective and passion, and I'm excited to see what will come next.

- Judith Lewis, fitness coach

"BEST BOOK EVER... EVERYONE NEEDS A COPY"

"I am beside myself with joy. The first few words of this book literally set me ablaze. I was tormented in my job and had been crying out to God for weeks. The minute I began reading, I was flooded with His guidance. This book is world class and I believe it will bring so much fruit. Honestly, I am a reader, I gobble books, but this is the best book ever! Truly, this needs to go global.
Sarah-Jane has a way of writing that makes the reader so hungry. This is not just about business either, everyone needs to have a copy of this book in their hand."

- Janet McCree, new business owner

"LET THIS BE A BOOK THAT HELPS YOU TAKE THAT FIRST STEP INTO YOUR FUTURE."

I love the heart and motivation of both this book and the author Sarah Jane. I have known and been the pastor of SJ and her husband Matt for many years and through many season of their lives. Her passion is to see people grow into the potential that they have and, more importantly, into the purpose that God has called them to.

This book will challenge and inspire you to "give it a go".

The New Testament is full of women and men who realised that their calling was to use their finances to see the kingdom of God expanded, the church to grow and "no unmet need" among them. This book will help you realise that potential in your life. Don't let it be just another book you read and put aside, let it be a book that helps you take that first step into your future.

- Pastor Jon Cook, Hillsong Newcastle

About the Author:

Sarah-Jane Ethan

SJ is a multiple-business owning entrepreneur of almost 10 years, and an international business coach. She has a natural instinct for sales and marketing and an infectious enthusiasm for business strategy. She lives in Newcastle with her husband Matt and their 'half-dog' cat Jeremy, and is an active member of her home-church, Hillsong Newcastle.

"When I first started in business, I did not have a clue what I was doing! I never dreamt that my businesses would grow so well or become international so quickly, or that Matt and I would end up with business coaching clients in seven countries and counting. I honestly believe this success has been propelled by the biblical principles we have fought to keep as our foundation, together with a determination to learn and grow. My desire is to pass this on to you, so that you can see unprecedented success in your business too. Through generating finance we can, not only live amazing lives ourselves but also, facilitate the message of hope and new life in Jesus to those who need Him.
Let's go and build the Kingdom one customer at a time!"

SJ x

Dedication

To my amazing parents, Pete & Fran.
For introducing me to God, showing me how to live 'sold-out'
for him, raising me to be confident and creative and kind,
giving me my first business idea and always supporting me in
every way you can. You are parents beyond compare!
I am who I am because of you.

To my hero husband Matt.
For supporting my dreams, giving me freedom to be myself,
teaching me to rest and inviting me to do this adventure of life
with you. I couldn't do anything I do without you.

To my pastors Jon & Dee.
For creating such an exceptional environment for us to know
God and grow in our purpose. Thank you for being
awe-inspiring examples of a life dedicated to Christ.
It is our honour to serve under you and alongside you.
You are the reason we stay in Newcastle.

A CIP catalogue record for this title is available from the British Library
ISBN 978-1-9164500-0-4

Unless otherwise state, all scripture quotations are taken from THE HOLY BIBLE, NEW INTERNATIONAL VERSION®, NIV® Copyright © 1973, 1978, 1984, 2011 by Biblica, Inc.® Used by permission. All rights reserved.

Scripture quotations marked MSG are taken from The Message. Copyright © 1993, 1994, 1995, 1996, 2000, 2001, 2002. Used by permission of NavPress Publishing Group.

Scripture quotations marked NLT are taken from the Holy Bible, New Living Translation, copyright © 1996, 2004, 2015. Used by permission of Tyndale House Publishers, Inc., Carol Stream, Illinois 60188. All rights reserved.

Scripture quotations marked TPT are taken from The Passion Translation®. Copyright © 2017 by BroadStreet Publishing® Group, LLC. Used by permission. All rights reserved. thePassionTranslation.com

Scripture quotations marked NKJV are taken from the New King James Version®. Copyright © 1982 by Thomas Nelson. Used by permission. All rights reserved.

Scripture quotations marked GW are taken from GOD'S WORD®, © 1995 God's Word to the Nations. Used by permission of Baker Publishing Group.

Scripture quotations marked with ESV are from the ESV® Bible (The Holy Bible, English Standard Version®) Copyright © 2001 by Crossway, a publishing ministry of Good News Publishers. Used by permission. All rights reserved."

Scripture quotations marked with CSB are from The Christian Standard Bible. Copyright © 2017 by Holman Bible Publishers. Used by permission.

Scripture quotations marked with CEV are from Contemporary English Version® Copyright © 1995 American Bible Society. Used with Permission. All rights reserved.

Scripture quotations marked with ISV are taken from The Holy Bible: International Standard Version® Release 2.1 Copyright © 1996-2012 The ISV Foundation ALL RIGHTS RESERVED INTERNATIONALLY.

Scripture quotations marked with KJV are taken from the King James Bible. Public Domain.

Cover image by Dominik-Schroder

Special Thanks

Thank you to all my clients and customers throughout the years who have allowed me to do what I love whilst serving them. Thank you also to all my faithful friends who have supported and encouraged me, hounded me to write this book, spent hours proof-reading and have given me the confidence to reach out to others with my story.

Special thanks to
Janet McCree, Brad Smith, Sandy Iles, Judith Lewis, Lindy Rogers, Angelina Ritchie-Smith, Fiona NG, Katie Etherton, Andrew Spence, Stephen Cook, Spider, Jack Wood, Amy Penberthy, Alison Dicken and Kate Hoggett for providing me with a crucial test audience and amazing early feedback.

An extra special thank you to my editors:
Judith Antsy and Lindsay Bruce
for their selfless help and tireless hours editing and correcting.
Thank you for making sure this book makes sense!

Content

Preface

To the Dreamers, the Creatives, the Desperate and the Determined;

To the Tycoons, the Trying and the just plain Tired;

Whether Full-time, Part-time or Living with a dream;

Welcome to The Business of Blessing!

Whether you are self-employed through choice, necessity or accident, now is the time to discover God's biblical blueprint to start and grow a God-abundant business. A business that not only attracts God's blessing but can become a channel of His blessing to others.

We are living in scary times.
Gone are the days of a job for life, a guaranteed pension and the ability to fund a retirement through exponential house price increases. Mass unemployment, redundant higher education and disproportionately low salaries leave many families living hand-to-mouth with little left over for relaxation, generosity or retirement. Second incomes, passive incomes or independent

businesses have become modern-day necessities, however Christians are being left behind. Through lack of confidence, fear of failure or a wrong understanding of wealth, many Christians feel unable to pursue their God-given earning potential to the fullest.

But we are also living in exciting times.
The opportunities for entrepreneurial business have never been easier! It has never been so easy to start a business from home, from scratch and with minimal training. Never before, in the history of the planet, has there been easier access to the international market or the ability to connect with high volumes of niché clients. The ability to create affordable advertising, access affordable design services and a wealth of available expertise in any industry means that even the most nervous of new entrepreneur can quickly and easily begin a business of their own.

With earning potentials higher than ever, significant salaries can be achieved with minimal investment compared to their historical counterparts. Gone are the days of bank loans, extortionate TV advertising and travelling salesmen, having been replaced with the ability to access the entire world audience at the touch of a button and for the price of a coffee. Never has there been a more perfect time to explore your entrepreneurial potential, increase your earning, improve your well-being and contribute to the kingdom on a significant level.

But... before you run out and quit your day job, let's first take a journey through the foundations of 'The Business of Blessing'.
My name is Sarah-Jane Ethan and I am a multiple business-owning entrepreneur and international business coach. I am also a committed Christian and passionate about financing the

Kingdom of God through supporting entrepreneurs like you to create wildly profitable and purposeful businesses. I honestly believe that Christians— who are inspired and equipped to step out into successful entrepreneurial business, with a passion to resource the local church— will help shape the financial future of the church.

I love the church, and have been a committed, active member ever since I became a Christian at the tender age of four years old. The church is God's solution for a hurting world but, although the gospel is free, it is never cheap. It costs money to reach others and create an environment for them to connect and grow. My passion is that— through practical, time-honoured business advice and inspirational biblical instruction, I can help you create a business that is as successful as possible. A business that both attracts God's blessing and can *be* a blessing.

A business that can prosper as soon as possible through God's very own biblical blueprint.

Welcome to 'The Business of Blessing'

Chapter 1

<u>Now is the Time</u>

Unlocking Your God-Given Potential

So this must be how Robinson Crusoe felt.

It was 2002 and I was on the adventure of a life time; hiking knee deep down a jungle river with 22 other explorers. It was heaven! I felt like an explorer of old, finding hidden pockets of God's creation, never seen before by another living soul. All was going well until we arrived at a 12 metre waterfall.

"Would anyone like to jump off?" asked the guide. *"If you do, just keep your shoes on or the impact will shatter your feet. You must also jump here and only here because, just below the surface, there are two hidden rock shelves and they'll probably kill you if you hit them. But in the middle, just there..."* He said, pointing ambiguously with his hand into the thundering torrent below, *"... there is a narrow gauge just wide enough to land in, and then you will be ok."*

I looked around at my fellow explorers as they slowly started to back away from the kind offer to dance with death. There were only 5 of us who jumped that day and I was the only girl. As I stepped up for my turn, I peered over the edge at the minimal chance of survival below. It was much scarier than I imagined!

I stopped myself mid-thought.

'I can't think about this, I have to just do it. If I think about it too much, I won't do it, I have to just jump." So I stepped back, cleared my head and took a running leap...

Till the day I die, I will never forget the sickening feeling of dread as my feet left the safety of the rock edge. 'What have I done??' I thought, in my brief moment of suspension before plunging to my fate.

I screamed the entire way down!

As I emerged back out of the waters below, I was still screaming but this time with pure exhilarated joy! "That was AMAZING!" I yelled. "I want to do it again!" And I ran straight back up and did again... twice!

This is exactly how it can feel when God calls you into a new season of challenge and risk, but the call is there none-the-less. As I read my Bible one day, these words practically smacked me in the face;

"Your work produced by faith,
Your labour motivated by love
And your endurance inspired by hope..."
1 Thessalonians 1:3 (CSB)

Work produced by faith? What exactly does that mean?

...immediately my mind floated over a dozen other verses of faith, finally resting on;

"Without faith it is impossible to please God..."
Hebrews 11:6

I pondered again, with those ancient words, "*Your work produced by faith...*" echoing around my spirit.

So our work (or job) can please or displease God depending on the faith it takes to do it? The daily challenge of faith in God's goodness, His provision and the responsibility to use our time, energy and talents for maximum reward.

My stomach churned with a mixture of challenge and excitement as I faced, as we all do, the uncomfortable question: Is my current work (my job) a product of faith or a product of fear?

Am I staying in my current employment because it's safe?

Because with a regular and predictable income I don't need to look to God for my daily bread?

Do I secretly like or crave the freedom to settle into a daily monotony of mindless work because it requires little in terms of real faith for God's provision?

Do I have a calling on my life to create, to achieve or to BE more, but that calling has been drowned out by the desire to live a safe life and avoid all risk of failure?

I mean, life is hard enough already! Is it really wrong to want to avoid the fear and uncertainty of stepping into uncharted territory? Surely God doesn't mean that I should step into a situation where every day is an exercise of faith in trusting His provision and His enabling through me? I thought trusting God was about seeking the most comfortable life possible, free from risk and challenge?

But the reality is very clear; without faith it is impossible to please God. If we are actively avoiding the fear of new beginnings, or unwilling to push ourselves beyond of our own ability into a place of dependence on God, we can never please Him in the area of our work.

'But surely it is sinful to desire more!' I hear you cry.

'Isn't greedy to be discontented with a mediocre or unsatisfying job?'

'It is pride to think that I could be capable of more or that God could open doors of opportunity for me that have not appeared to open for others!'

Or the most common excuse for avoiding the step of faith into the unknown; 'I need a sign from God to know if it is His will for me to step out in faith.'

But the bible says;

"In the past God spoke to our ancestors through the prophets
at many times and in various ways,
but in these last days he has spoken to us by his Son."
Hebrews 1:1-2

So, let's stop for one minute and explore the words of Jesus himself.

You see, often we don't need the variety of supernatural ways that God has spoken in the past if Jesus has already directly given us the instruction, the challenge and the direction that we need.

Let's look at one of the most confusing and challenging parables that Jesus told, the parable of the Talents:

"It's also like a man going off on an extended trip. He called his
servants together and delegated responsibilities.
To one he gave five thousand dollars, to another two thousand, to a
third one thousand, depending on their abilities.
Then he left.

Right off, the first servant went to work and doubled his master's investment. The second did the same.
But the man with the single thousand dug a hole and carefully buried his master's money.

After a long absence, the master of those three servants came back and settled up with them. The one given five thousand dollars showed him how he had doubled his investment.
His master commended him: 'Good work! You did your job well. From now on be my partner.'

"The servant with the two thousand showed how he also had doubled his master's investment. His master commended him: 'Good work! You did your job well. From now on be my partner.'

"The servant given one thousand said, 'Master, I know you have high standards and hate careless ways, that you demand the best and make no allowances for error. I was afraid I might disappoint you, so I found a good hiding place and secured your money. Here it is, safe and sound down to the last cent.'

"The master was furious.
'That's a terrible way to live!
It's criminal to live cautiously like that!
If you knew I was after the best, why did you do less than the least? The least you could have done would have been to invest the sum with the bankers, where at least I would have gotten a little interest.

"'Take the thousand and give it to the one who risked the most. And get rid of this "play-it-safe" who won't go out on a limb. Throw him out into utter darkness.'"
Matthew 25: 14-30 (MSG)

Many people struggle with this parable because it seems to be promoting greed. Is the landowner greedy and only interested in wealth? Why does he scold the worker who hid his money, surely that was the safe option? Surely it was wisdom to seek minimal risk in case of failure?

Why does he promote the worker who took the greatest risk? The ones who could have lost it all? The ones who acted without fear in order to gain the greatest reward?

If the landowner (who represents God) favours this fearless pursuit of maximum reward, then what does God require of us in our lives?

The landowner was looking for something from his workers. He wanted to see who could be trusted to have drive and ambition. To see who would be focused and fearless. To discover who would be strategic and passionate about creating the greatest reward from the investment that he made.

If they could be trusted with a little, then he could entrust them with a lot.

It is worth adding that financial gain through self-employment and business is not the only way to faithfully invest our time, talents and abilities for maximum reward. The full-time mum investing in her children can also be discharging her duty, as can the full-time pastor, charity worker, carer and those employed in their dream job.

I am speaking specifically to those of you who know that you have the entrepreneurial itch. Those that long to build their own

21

business or are faced with the necessity to do so through circumstances, unexpected opportunity or plain curiosity (which is just as valid a reason by the way!)

It could be argued that by seeking a low-risk/low-reward life we are actually burying God's investment in the ground too. God has invested dreams, desires, passions and abilities within you that he wants you to use for maximum reward. We can too easily justify our avoidance of any possible failure as prudence or wisdom but God doesn't call us to avoid risk. He calls us to live fearless lives full of faith! To be dominated by the fear of failure, to the point that we never even try, is the exact opposite to living a fearless life of faith.

By the way, this still applies even if you feel you have had disappointments in the past. Perceived past failure does not make you exempt from the call to live a life of faith! God calls us to be brave, to believe Him for impossible things and to care more about His opinion than the opinions of those around us.
The Bible is absolutely bursting with inspirational stories of those who stepped out in faith against all the odds. I defy you to find one single verse that commends the pursuit of a safe, comfortable, risk-free life that requires minimal faith.

My husband, Matt, has a question that he asks himself whenever he is faced with a new challenge or crossroad decision: "What is the scariest option?"
He then challenges himself to choose this option.
The scariest option is usually the one that you do not feel capable of achieving without God's help. It requires the most amount of faith.
This is a good choice.
This is the perfect choice!

God is calling us to live a life of faith and you can't do this if you always choose the easiest path that requires the least amount of faith! By avoiding risk, we are actually echoing the words of the cautious worker who said in v 24-25: "<you> make no allowances for error. I was afraid I might disappoint you."

Do we really think that God is so strict that he would be more concerned with the mistakes we make through inexperience or excitement than the obedience and faith we were trying to please him with? Do we really think that God is unable or unwilling to redeem any mistake that we may make and turn it around for good?

God once gave me a picture of a child running towards their father but falling through their over-enthusiasm and inexperience. The father wasn't cross, of course not! His heart was overflowing with pride and love to know that his child's focus and desire had been for him. He ran to his child to sooth and carry them, laughing while he said, *"It doesn't matter that you fell, I just love that you tried."*

So it is with God. We need to have a fresh revelation of the father heart of God. He is more interested in our energetic desire to exercise reckless faith than any mistake we may make along the way. I am not saying that it will always been plain sailing or that we should ignore our God-given wisdom and common sense, but if you are prayerfully stepping out in faith, as wisely as you know how, God is more pleased with your effort to believe him for the impossible than the actual action you are taking. In this respect, I would argue that any risk you take pleases God if it done with a deep, excited and convicted belief in God's goodness, faithfulness and power.

It is always the right time to step out in faith.

23

If you do inadvertently make an unwise decision there is no reason to fear God's retribution, leaving you to failure, poverty and disgrace. If you were stepping out in faith with a heart to please him, do you really think God will want to punish you for trying to believe, with all your heart, that he is who he says he is? Of course not!

If you have made a slightly wrong decision, God is more than able to give you a gentle nudge, closing doors and open others to redirect your path. A moving ship is far easier to steer than a static one.

Equally he can redeem any mistake and turn it round for good if we trust him and keep moving forward as best we know how.

He can restore relationships, replenish your bank balance, revive your reputation and breathe new life into apparent endings.

In God, nothing is wasted.

No mistake, apparent failure, financial ruin, misunderstanding, lost reputation or disappointment is ever permanent so what do you have to lose? If God can restore and redeem any action that you take and will bless and honour the faith you show, then what is holding you back from taking that leap of faith?

We may declare with our mouth that God is the God of the impossible but we will demonstrate through our life choices whether we actually believe this to be true. By choosing the safest, easiest options we are actually declaring our lack of faith in God's goodness, generosity and miraculous power. We are declaring with our feet that we do not believe that God is as good as he says he is or that he is as powerful as he says he is. We are declaring that we do not believe him to be our provider, our loving Father and Lord over all things... can you see why we can never please God this way?!

"Faith by itself, if it is not accompanied by action, is dead."
James 2v17

So herein lies one of the keys to experiencing abundance in your business; have reckless faith.
Be brave.
Be expectant.
Pray and plan for the impossible.

"...I will show you my faith by my actions."
James 2v18 (ISV)

God LOVES it!
I mean he REALLY loves it! His heart is so swollen with pride to see how dedicated we are to create the maximum return for the talent, ability and time resource he has given us. God has placed desires and visions in your heart. They may feel so impossible, selfish or scary that you dare not even acknowledge that they are there.
But if you quiet the fear, ignore the rational thought that says you could never achieve it and reject the guilt that says you are not allowed to dream big, you will find that deep within you there is a longing to do more, to achieve more and to BE more.
The longing to be successful, to excel and to achieve. The desire to pursue your passions and satisfy your curiosity. The desire to turn hobbies into a way of life and turn ideas into reality. The desire to innovate, to communicate or to simply feel in control of your own schedule. The desire for more family time, more financial freedom and more leisure time. The desire to feel like you have 'made' something of your life.

None of this is wrong!

These are God-given desires. It is the kind of drive that Jesus himself promoted in the parable of the talents. God wants us to make full use of our abilities to learn, to create and to connect with others. Money, success and business achievements are not wrong if they are achieved through honest means and with consideration for others. What we do with our wealth is where our responsibility lies.

Just like the parable of the talents, if your aim is to dedicate your increase back to God, to be used for him, then God will bless your efforts and your business will prosper.

We have a primary responsibility to meet the needs of the poor, to show compassion, servanthood and outrageous generosity. But we also have the equally important responsibility to create this wealth in the first place and this is where creating an abundant business comes in!

Through self-employment you not only have the opportunity to create work that uniquely fits your priorities, lifestyle and passions but there is also no upper limit to what you can earn. You have the opportunity to create a business that far exceeds your own needs so you can provide considerable financial blessings to those around you and fund the mission of your local church.

You can't give out of what you don't have!

You can't be abundantly generous unless you have abundant finance to do this. God can't use you to meet the needs of those around you unless you have first accepted his finances to be able to do this.

Think about when you have seen God provide in your own life, whether through financial provision, gifted resources or open doors of opportunity. How was it delivered? Did it drop out of the sky or was it handed to you by another human-being faithfully discharging his calling to be generous? In the vast majority of cases, it will have been given to you by another person.

This is God's preferred method of provision. God is a God of inclusion and commission. He uses each one of us to be the vessels by which he reaches and meets the needs of the world. Most of us are more than happy to pray for provision for ourselves yet don't feel in faith to pray for enough excess resource to be able to meet someone else's needs too. Why is that? Why do we feel so comfortable to pray for money for our own specific need yet uncomfortable to pray for excess wealth to meet the needs of many others?

This is why the landowner was so cross with the worker that took the least risk and was happy with no additional reward, because he did not create any excess resource. God is looking for us to do more, to achieve more and ultimately to EARN more because with this additional resource he can do so much more through your life for his kingdom. Wanting to earn in excess is a God-honouring desire if your end goal is to be more useful to the kingdom of God. This type of drive is blessed by God with abundance.

This is your "**labour promoted by love**".

This abundant finance will not drop into your lap, that is not how it works! You must labour for it. It will take hard work. God does not reward your prayer for finance if you are praying from a cocoon of risk-free, faithless, motionless safety. Faith does not mean believing that God can do it miraculously without any risk-taking action on your part. Equally, God will not reward the prayer that says, "Please show the provision first and THEN I will take action."

This is not faith.

It is not faith to only step out when you feel certain of success, this is just common sense! Faith is being certain of what we cannot see (Hebrews 11v1). If you are expecting God to do all the hard work so you can simply and easily step from one comfort zone to the next, you are going to be bitterly disappointed. You will spend your whole life frustrated about why the doors of opportunity appear to open for everyone else but not for you!

No, it is going to be scary. There will be risk so great it will threaten to keep you awake at night with worry. You will battle daily to keep your eyes on Christ, to believe in his ability to provide for the needs of your family and to open the doors that need to be opened. There will be sacrifice. You will feel inadequate, under-qualified and embarrassed. You will cry, you will worry and you will be forced into a place of total dependence on God.

...But, it is in this place of desperation you will discover the deepest levels of God's peace and hope. This is why he is calling you here. It is only in this place of total dependence that you will learn what faith really means. You will learn how to take your disappointment to God and exchange it for his hope and joy.

And you will know his reward.

"So do not throw away your confidence;
it will be richly rewarded.
You need to persevere so that when you have done the will of God you
will receive what he has promised."
Hebrews 10v35-36

Through the parable of the talents, Jesus is promising that your faith, your bravery and your reckless belief that God can achieve great things through you, will be rewarded. The more you show that you can be trusted to plan for success, to focus on a bigger picture and invest your time, energy and talent for maximum reward, the more God can trust you with. Your resources and supernatural opportunity will increase as God trusts you to be faithful with whatever he gives you.

You will know God's supernatural provision that goes far beyond what you ever thought you could achieve. You will be a living, walking, breathing testimony to what God can do through an individual who is prepared to say 'No' to fear and step into the unknown. You will know the unparalleled ecstasy of success and satisfy your God-given desires to prosper, create and rest.

God is calling you to choose your "work produced by faith". Not tomorrow, not the next year, not when your mortgage is paid off... now!

Today!

You are at a crossroads: will you take the easy road that allows you to live a low-risk/low-reward life, or will you accept God's challenge to face your fears head on and fulfil your potential. Will you accept his hand as he leads you into terrifyingly exciting places? Into a place where success is won through error, failure and persistence. Where faith is grown, like a muscle, through tears of desperation and the overwhelming pain of longing. Where you learn to live in joy and peace no matter what challenges you face, until at last you see the fruit of your labour and your faith rewarded.

This is your "**endurance inspired by hope.**"

The promise is to see your faith-filled, fearless efforts multiplied in such a way that you are not only able to provide for the needs of your family but provide for the needs of many families more through the abundant resources that God will give you.

Will you step out today?

"To him who is able to do immeasurably more than we ask or imagine, According to his power... to him be the glory... for ever and ever, amen."
Ephesians 3v 20-21

Chapter 2

The First Step

<u>Building a Foundation</u>

Katie-Ann:
The alarm sounded. 5.45am... again.
Every day; the same routine.
Katie-Ann dutifully trudged to the office, took her place at the desk and began the predictable morning task of placating her ever-demanding email inbox. The sound of a blue jay caught her attention, drawing her eyes out of the window to the glorious mid-summer's day. For one blissful moment she daydreamed about having her own business one day. The freedom, the creativity, the fulfilment... one day! One day.

Ben:
Ben was fresh out of university with high hopes of the managerial position he could surely achieve with such good grades. The bubble quickly burst with only one glance at the depressingly low-salary/high-demand jobs available in his industry, perpetuated by the vast quantities of desperate new

graduates. Was there another way, other than to joining the long line of hopefuls fighting for each position?

Karen:
The excitement was building; this was Karen and Pete's first baby.
But as Karen's due date sped increasingly close she began to feel less and less enthralled at the idea of returning to her current job. What if she could create her own work? Maybe even work from home? Create a flexible schedule to fit around the needs of her future family? Was that even possible?

John:
32 years of faithful service and this was how it all ended?!
John gazed numbly at the impersonal letter, coldly explaining that his services could no longer be afforded and he was being made redundant. "Redundant"?! Is that what he was now? Who else would hire him at 52 years old? With decades of experience and full of life and passion, John was not ready to slip into his tartan slippers just yet! He had never considered becoming a private consultant in his industry but maybe this was the push he needed?

I wonder what stage of life you are in right now? Is this the life you dreamt of? A life of excitement, adventure and choice?
What if there was another way? What if the freedom and fulfilment you crave could actually become a reality?
Self-employment offers the flexibility to create your own schedule, set your own processes and customer service standards, and decide your own income. But even more excitingly, self-employment gives you the opportunity to earn significantly over and beyond your own needs to become a

kingdom-builder; financing the kingdom of God in a way that changes lives all over the world.

There are three main reasons that a person can find themselves pursuing an independent self-employed business:

- **Accident:** Discovering a profitable idea, a niche in the market or a need in the society that is not yet provided for.
- **Necessity:** Unemployment, redundancy, insufficient salary or lack of work/life balance.
- **Passion:** The overwhelming desire to create something unique, to be in control, to turn a hobby into an income or to simply increase their earning potential.

For myself, I became self-employed by accident more than a decade ago. I was the first member of my immediate family to be officially self-employed. I spent hours pouring over the various government website pages and was a weekly caller to their self-employed telephone helpline, as I desperately tried to figure out what it meant to be self-employed and how to do it well.

My journey took me by surprise.
I went from being an intensive care nurse en route to the African mission field to a multiple-business-owning entrepreneur and international business coach. I never saw it coming!
Let me give you the slightly scenic story to illustrate how cunningly God can monumentally redirect the course of your life with one seemingly insignificant moment. For me, that moment was when my best friend Abi told me that she was planning to move to abroad with her new husband for a year or two.

I said to my mum, "*I'm really going to miss her. I don't know what I will do without her!*"

"*Why don't you take this opportunity to have an adventure of your own?*" she casually suggested.

"*Hmm,*" I thought, "*what would I do if I wasn't nursing?*"

My mind immediately thought back to a Christian hip hop youth worker's academy I had noticed years before. I had always dreamt of doing it but it didn't seem very practical or in keeping with my plans to nurse on the African mission field. But it looked like great fun and it was only five months long. I'd be back before I knew it... or so I thought!

So, much to the amusement of my colleagues, I packed up everything I owned and headed off on my five month adventure.

(Interestingly, I thought my colleagues would think I was mad but every single one of them was jealous. They all said to me, "*I've always dreamed of doing X, Y or Z but just never had the guts to do it!*" I wonder how many others are secretly living with regret and unfulfilled dreams?)

It was at this academy that I first met singing teacher Heather Baker, and a completely revolutionary singing system. I had always been a good singer but within minutes Heather got me singing in ways I never thought I could. She showed me that God had given my voice far more potential than I had ever realised.

Fast forward 2 years to Newcastle, north-east England, and I was facing the end of my time with a Christian hip-hop Youth outreach band. I began to consider my obvious next employment options. Should I return to nursing?

I casually mentioned to my mum how frustrating it was not having any singing teachers in the North East teaching this same revolutionary singing system.

In all seriousness, my Mum suggested, "Why don't YOU teach it then?"

"Me??" I recoiled. "I couldn't... I mean... I wouldn't know how... where would I even start? No, that's not for me."

We ended the call and I thought I had laid the idea to rest but it began to grow in my mind without me even realising. I was faced with a potential niché in my local market. A need that was not yet provided for. Rather than complaining that there was no one filling the position, no one to serve my needs, I could be the one to step up and begin to serve the needs of everyone else. Could I really do it?

I knew the system worked, I knew my voice had changed beyond recognition and I knew that the singers of the North East needed to experience this too.

Suddenly my dogged determination kicked in: I'm going to do it!

And that was the start.

With the same determined focus of a ship powering through a blinding storm, I began the all-consuming process of vocal coach training. I worked 10 hours a day during the final months of my youth worker job and then invested in several hours of private study each evening too.

With absolutely no capital, I bought what I could afford: a £5 second-hand mini keyboard with a broken sound-card (the only "sound" it would play was the trumpets!) I then spent hours teaching myself, by ear, how to play the variety of complicated scales and arpeggios needed for my upcoming teaching debut.

Without even the funds for a keyboard stand, I precariously balanced my keyboard on top of my ironing board and engaged my first paying singing client: my mum.

With the money I earned I bought a cheap keyboard stand and I was off...

Thanks to a unique advertising angle I had created (which I'll tell you about later) I quickly went from a nobody, with no qualifications or experience, to one of the most sought-after coach in the area. Within a very short space of time I had a home studio, tripled my prices and was charging twice as much as almost every other teacher in the area. I was also permanently fully booked and had over 100 people on the waiting list. I was earning much higher than my employed counterparts and I was in control of my own timetable and working from home in my slippers!

This was just the first of my entrepreneurial businesses and I was hooked! There was no way I could ever go back to being employed; being told what to do and when to do it. Being frustrated with inefficient systems and poor customer service but unable to do anything about it.

Building businesses unexpectedly became my passion and within just a few years my new businesses were taking me around the world in a way I never dreamt was possible. I honestly feel like I am living the dream!

I often think back and imagine my life had I stayed in nursing and how different it would be. Nursing is an amazing calling and no society could function without the army of faithful people serving others in hospitals and other equally vital roles, but I think back specifically to my colleagues who are still living with regret. Over 10 years later, with neither the confidence nor the courage to take the risk and pursue their dreams, they are still slaving through gruelling shifts and infuriating red tape. I feel so overwhelmed with awe and gratitude for the freedom and adventure that my new life has brought, and I know that this can be your life too.

The First Step

I am excited for the things that God has spoken into your heart as we explored the first chapter and our calling and responsibility to live a life of reckless faith. I believe and pray that God has reignited old dreams, or planted new ones within your heart, but don't run out and quit your day job just yet! Passion and calling alone are not enough to create a successful business, we need a plan. We must be wise and strategic if we are going to generate the greatest return on God's investment. There is a perfect example of this in Joshua 8. As the Israelites advanced into the promised land they came upon the city of Ai. God said to Joshua,

> "Do not be afraid; do not be discouraged.
> Take the whole army with you, and go up and attack Ai.
> For I have delivered into your hands the king of Ai, his people, his city and his land."
> **Joshua 8:1**

This may be the place you are in right now; you are aware of the passions and callings in your heart, and have a new confidence to believe in God's promise to prosper you. You are ready to act with faith and courage, just as Joshua was. But Joshua didn't simply run head-long at the city of Ai, he created a strategy... a really clever one!

> "So Joshua and the whole army moved out to attack Ai.
> He chose thirty thousand of his best fighting men and sent them out at night with these orders:
> 'Listen carefully. You are to set an ambush behind the city.

Don't go very far from it. All of you be on the alert.
I and all those with me will advance on the city, and when the men come
out against us, as they did before, we will flee from them.
They will pursue us until we have lured them away from the city, for they
will say, 'They are running away from us as they did before.'
So when we flee from them, you are to rise up from ambush and take
the city. The Lord your God will give it into your hand. "
Joshua 8:3-7

This was a genius plan. Joshua understood of the psychology of the people of Ai. He knew what assumptions they would make, and how to gain the advantage. The success of his new plan also rested on the disaster of their previous defeat, which is another encouraging reminder that nothing is ever wasted with God. Joshua used this past mistake to his advantage. He drew the enemy out of the city by pretending to run away in defeat, as they had last time. He knew the people of Ai would be feeling cocky and, in their delight at another supposed victory, would leave the city unguarded. His hidden army could then capture the city behind their backs.

I love this story because it highlights so perfectly, the importance of creating strategy. God gives promises, and ultimately brings the victory, but his promises rely on our faith-filled action. When it comes to answering the call of your heart to pursue self-employment and create a business of your own, there is no greater, faith-filled action than creating a plan; a strategy for success.

That is what we are going to do throughout the rest of this book. By the end of this book, and through the study guide and business plan available at www.businessofblessing.com, we will create a strategy for success for you. A methodical plan

38

that will allow you to pursue the promise of God on your life with wisdom and courage. My deepest desire is that your business will grow and prosper as quickly as possible, because I know that this is God's desire for you.

Whether you are starting a new business or looking to "scale up" an existing one, the first step is to identify what the "next level" looks like for your business. To do this I have created the Potential Profit Pyramid (PPP).

Potential Profit Pyramid

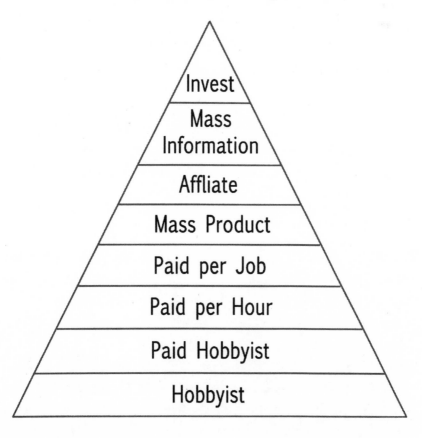

The earning potential increases with each level of the PPP however, as the level of reward increases, so does the level of financial risk and effort.

Therefore, this is a very personal decision with no right or wrong answer.

Whatever you are selling, your End Commercial Product (ECP) is simply the product or service of value that your customer is purchasing. Because this varies wildly from industry to industry, we will refer to your product or service as your End Commercial Product or your "ECP" from now on.

Hobbyist

It is really important to include this as the first stage of self-employment because many people mistake a hobby for a new business. There is absolutely nothing wrong with having a hobby, we all need them, but it is important to know where the line between a hobby and a business lies. As a hobbyist, you fund this activity yourself. You may earn a small amount but it does not cover the full expense of creating or delivering your service/product. It is extremely exciting to receive any money for an activity that you enjoy but it does not become a viable business idea, until you are able to cover your costs and generate a liveable salary.

I once had a friend who excitedly told me about her new cake-making business. She told me that business was booming, she had so many orders she couldn't keep up with them, so she was thinking of converting her garage into a fully-stocked commercial kitchen.

"That's amazing!" I replied, *"How much are you charging?"*

She looked at me confused and said, *"Oh I'm not charging anything, I pay for the ingredients myself."*

It was my turn to look confused.

I did not have the heart to burst her bubble by saying, "Well you don't really have a business, what you have is a very expensive hobby!"

Of course she had orders coming out of her ears, she was giving away high-quality, made-to-order cakes! I had the mind to order several myself!

Do not mistake an opportunist for a genuine customer. Real customers (and real friends) are those who value your product enough to open their wallets and pay you what you are worth.

Do not mistake a "business" for a very expensive hobby. If you are not earning enough to cover your production costs then you are sustaining a hobby. There is absolutely nothing wrong with having a hobby and it is absolutely okay to keep your craft at the hobby level if you wish. We all need hobbies and relaxing interests outside of work, but do not mistake your hobby for a business— it is a very expensive mistake to make!

Paid Hobbyist

Equally deceptive is the position of paid hobbyist. As a hobbyist, you fund your own hobby; as a paid hobbyist, someone else funds it. As a paid hobbyist your customers will be covering your production and delivery costs only. If there is any extra, it will amount to little more than pocket money or a little extra spending money.

The very first question I ask anyone wanting to start a business is, 'what do you want or need this business to be? Are you doing this for the love of it and happy with a small supplementary income, or do you want a full-time business?'

Do you like the idea of having no pressure to monetise your craft, creating intensive marketing and sales strategies etc? Are you happy to have a handful of clients, each paying a small amount, to offset your minimal running costs?

If you like the idea of keeping your new business at a 'cottage industry' size; earning enough to cover your costs and giving you a small amount of additional income, this is absolutely fine! There is nothing wrong with being a paid hobbyist if you are wanting to do this purely for fun and relaxation. Getting paid to do something you love is valid, as long as you decide, from the start, that you are not aiming to give up your day job. You must be clear that you want to keep this as a low-risk/low-income, relaxing, paid hobby.

The frustration will only come if you are hoping this will become a full-time income or even a substantial second income. If you need or want to build a career and create a life-sustaining income, then you can't afford to structure your business at the paid hobbyist level.

To determine if you are a paid hobbyist you must first calculate the basic expenses of your ECP. This is the cost of your raw materials, processes, websites, vehicle running costs etc. Once you have offset whatever you have earned against these basic expenses, there will be very little left over to compensate the amount of time it has taken you to create or deliver your product or service. If there is no money left over, after you have covered the cost of creating your ECP, then you are unable to pay yourself a salary and are, therefore, a paid hobbyist.

If you do have a little additional money, that is great. To calculate whether you are still a paid hobbyist, you must now divide the profit between the number of hours it has taken to plan, shop for materials, take orders, create and deliver your ECP. How much does your profit equal when divided into an hourly rate to cover every hour spent on your business? Your minimum hourly wage should be roughly 2.5-5 times the national minimum wage in order to be viable as a full-time self-employed income. This not only includes every client-facing hour but also every hour spent on preparation, research and development also. We'll discuss this is more detail later.

By the Hour

At this stage, you are paid by the hour for the work that you do. A client who is looking to engage your service would receive a quote along the lines of:

X hours at X amount per hour = X total cost.

There are many areas of service that prefer this payment structure (coaches, consultations, tradesmen etc) and the hourly rate of pay varies according to experience, confidence and industry expectation. The fact is, when paid by the hour, earning is limited to the amount of hours you are physically able to work. You can't easily increase your income without increasing the number of hours worked, which can negatively affect your family life and your physical/emotional wellbeing through stress and exhaustion. There can also be difficult conversations over further payment with your client if you are completing a long-term job that begins to require additional time through no fault of your own. Price increases can also be difficult to achieve, particularly if you have a regular clientele expecting a certain price. Finally, if you can't work for any reason through sickness or unexpected personal demands then you simply do not earn with a "pay by the hour" business.

By the Job

When you are self-employed and charging by the job, a client who is looking to engage your services will receive a quote along the lines of: X job required = X amount total cost, and the quote is inclusive of all costs. There is no discussion over your hourly rate, there is only a final price for the total ECP they require.

The benefit with this system is that you are less likely to have clients trying to drive down their quote by under-estimating the job's length or complexity. You can also add a contingency amount into the quote so that, should the job overrun, you can afford to work further without needing to negotiate further payment. With this higher, 'all inclusive' quote, you are more easily able to increase your prices over time, with little affect on your clientele, as the small increases are more negotiable compared to the larger final price.

Charging by the job also allows you to increase your profit margin, without increasing the quote, by increasing your skill and efficiency. As you become better and quicker at your job, your profit margin increases. This increasing your annual salary, without actually raising your client's quote. Everyone's a winner! Any ECP that can be described as "by this set time we will have achieved this result" can be charged by the job instead of by the hour.

Mass Product Sales

The next stage of the PPP is to sell a physical product at a mass availability level. In order for this to be different from the previous two stages, this product must be in mass production and, therefore, not directly dependent on your physical hours worked. Selling a physical product, through an automated production process, can significantly increase your earning potential because your profit is no longer dependent on the hours you can physically work, as you now have other workers or technology creating the ECP for you.

Once the ECP is in mass production, you have the potential to sell multiple products to simultaneous customers, thus increasing your earning potential. You have the ability to increase your income without directly increasing your personal exertion by simply increasing the sales of your independently replicable ECP. Your earning potential is no longer directly linked to the hours you work but is solely dependant on the number of customers who buy your product at any given time.

Affiliate Sales

An affiliate is someone who sells someone else's ECP on a commission-based system. This includes:

- online or physical agencies and directories.
- online or physical affiliate salesmen or processes.
- websites, blogs or video blogs generating revenue through sponsorship and advertising.

Being an affiliate in any industry has a higher earning potential because the affiliate absorbs none of the ECP production costs. There is no lengthy research, design and development stages. There is no on-going customer service. There are often minimal set-up costs and little-to-no risk involved. An affiliate simply takes an existing ECP and connects it with potential buyers on a commission-basis system.

The difficulty is that you will often be competing against many others wanting to be an affiliate for that same ECP and you will also be competing against the company itself. To become an affiliate, you must be confident that you can reach a new audience, in a more effective way than the original company could. The most profitable form of affiliate sales is to spot a new ECP before others do and therefore market it with minimal competition.

Mass Information Sales

Even more profitable than selling a physical, manufactured product is selling an information-based product. This means selling your knowledge or expertise in the form of pre-

prepared, mass-available coaching, education or training programmes. This includes:

- publications based on news, current affairs, international commentary, comedy, fashion, culture etc.
- education on industry processes, market strategy, efficiency increase and profit increase etc.
- lifestyle coaching, motivation, mentoring, support etc.
- support and education in health, fitness, fashion, relationships, parenting, creative design, sports, music, niche skills etc.

The list goes on.

The benefit of selling an information based product is that it greatly reduces your manufacturing costs. There is no expense required to buy raw materials or expensive construction processes. The only expense needed is the final packaging cost to deliver the ECP in an appealing, accessible and effective format.

You are selling the information in your head, the expertise you have gained through study, experience, trial and error. Because your physical production costs are much lower, there is less risk involved in starting an information-based business and, therefore, a greater possibility for profit. The whole profit is yours to keep, in contrast to an affiliate who might sell a similar product but for a smaller commission.

Investor

An investor is someone who invests money into an asset such as companies, inventions, stocks or property. The asset is predicted to increase in value over time due to external contributing factors such as economic changes, consumer demand or product development. As the asset increases in value the investor earns a passive income (an income not directly related to the investors personal time or energy) and this is why investment is the highest level in the effort-to-reward based PPP. There are, however, inherent risks with investing in an asset which is only *predicted* to appreciate in value. Due to unforeseen contributing factors such as company incompetency, economics changes or reduced demand, there is the chance that the investment may fail to yield any profit and may even lose money.

A wise investment principle is the 1% rule: aim to invest only 1% of your available capital in any high risk venture. This spreads the risk and provides a level of protection at this high risk/highest reward stage in the PPP.

"Invest in seven ventures, yes, in eight;
you do not know what disaster may come upon the land."
Ecclesiastes 11v 2

Be wise, cautious and balanced in your investments. As a Christian investor, your primary mission is not to make a quick buck by placing huge amount of money in uncertain ventures. Wise investment is simply looking to steward the resources at your disposal to create maximum reward, without being seduced by the promise of instant riches or gambling your investment on a single, untested venture.

This PPP is a hugely simplified version of the myriad of possible avenues for self-employment. There is no guaranteed return at each level— a person working by the hour may earn significantly more than an affiliate salesmen for example— success relies purely on the skill and determination of the business owner. There is no right or wrong stage and no stage is greater than another, it is merely a generalised indication of the earning potential.

The one thing the PPP also cannot account for is your passion. The best businesses are not borne out of a desire for profit alone, but from a passion for the product, a natural skill and a desire to serve the needs of others too. There is no right or wrong business model for your ECP, but the PPP is there should you be looking for ways to increase your earning potential and develop your business to the next level.

Chapter 3

<u>Finding Your Niche</u>

How to Get Your First Business Idea

It was a 6am on a crisp spring morning.
Propelled by the fresh enthusiasm of a young mind alive with
resolve and possibility, I slipped out of bed and crept through
the house, revelling in the satisfaction of being the first member
of my family awake and ready to "seize the day". Stepping out
into the frosty air in my joggers and fleece, I began pounding
the streets, driven by the dream of my new, fitter self. Only
moments into my early morning run I began to feel the
characteristic aching in my thighs, burning in my chest and the
throbbing of my cheeks. Suddenly all the romantic ideals I had
of a blissful morning jog evaporated in the light of the heart-
thumping, sweat-inducing reality. This was not fun at all!
My one hour running goal quickly reduced to intervals of two
minutes of light jogging interspersed with two minutes of
walking and 15 minutes later I was back in my room.
My cheeks were as red as cranberries and the throbbing lasted
for at least three hours (I was convinced I had burst some

blood vessels!) I don't recall if I went for another run the next day, but I am pretty sure that I did not.

Starting a new business is one of the most thrilling experiences there is. Bursting with the anticipation of success one can blissfully swim in a mental sea of dreams and potential. The possibility of earning a full-time salary from something that you love, being in control of your own schedule and the possibility of more rest and disposable income can create a heady cocktail.
Fuelled by such enthusiasm, why is it that around 60% of new business ventures fail within the first five years?
(Office of National Statistics, Business Demography Report 2016)

Many people start a business without realising they are doomed to fail. They think they are passionate about being an "entrepreneur" and creating a business for themselves but the primary question in their mind is, "How can I make the most amount of money with the smallest time and money investment?"
They look for get-rich-quick schemes, invest unwisely or simply choose an industry that they have no emotional connection with.
These businesses will always fail.
The moment it is not as easy as they expected, not as profitable as they hoped or requires more effort than they were prepared to give, they simply pack up and leave, and the investment is lost. This is the reality for the majority of new start-up businesses.
As my husband would say, "Entrepreneurs find a way forward when others can't. If it was easy there would be no need for them to be entrepreneurial. That's what being an entrepreneur means!"

This is actually good news for you and I, because, if the majority of new businesses fail, there is more room for your business to succeed. All you need is to be one of the few people who stick at it. If it was easy, everyone would be doing it and the competition would be so great that there would be no room left in the market for you. If the market was already completely saturated with thousands of others already doing the thing you want to do and succeeding at it, then who would your customers be?

Every market and industry has room for one more person, if they have the fresh determination, ideas, products and processes, to rise to the top. With fresh marketing, branding and efficiency there is absolutely no reason why your business cannot sail past those who have been established for decades.

Experience is not the thing that will propel a business forward, being established in an industry does not guarantee future success. Every industry changes over time with changes in consumer demand and new technologies. Businesses that do not adapt will always get left behind giving new businesses a chance to rise up in their place.

With the right tools, focus and skills a fledgling business can quickly surpass an old school one and any new entrepreneur can enter any industry they desire, no matter how competitive it may seem.

The only factor to success is the determination and ability to do what your competitors are doing, but do it better.

The key, to excelling at any business is remembering that your ECP is measured by the value it adds to your customer's life. Customers will pay for a product or service when they consider that the value of that product or service is greater than the money it will take to buy it.

If the ECP meets their expectation, they are happy customers; if the ECP exceeds their expectations then they will become "brand evangelists", actively recommending you to anyone who will listen.

When looking for your first business idea, the key question to ask is: What can I do to enrich the lives of others?

Answering this question can be hard, so I have created the discovery quiz below, to help you explore your potential.

The more you try to find answers, the more examples will spring to mind, so write down as many answers as you can possibly think of for each question. You may discover new ideas that you would not necessarily have ever thought of.

- **What qualifications do you have?** What industries have you worked or trained in? What skills, understanding or experience have you gained from this work?

- **What areas of the world interest you most?** This means you spend a large proportion of your relaxation time reading, researching or enjoying this. For example, this could be: travel, popular culture, current affairs, global politics, history, the arts, animal care, cooking, crafting, DIY, fashion, comedy or the natural world.

- **What hobbies/skills do you invest the most time mastering?** For example: playing an instrument, sports, art, linguistics, performance, carpentry, gardening, video gaming, creative skills, movies.

- **What social activities do you enjoy most?** This might be good food and drink, peace and nature, city living, social connections, organising events.

- **What natural qualities do you have?** Do you have organisational ability, analytical thinking, humour, confident presentation, adventurous spirit, compassion?

- **What need can you see in your current world?** This relates to inadequate services or products that are difficult to access, to use or are simply non-existent. This may be based on your own experience or those close to you. Can you see solutions? Can you bring services together to make them more complete? Can you start something that doesn't currently exists or make something that is easier to access, use or adapt?

- **What experience have you had that you can use to support others in?** Examples might include parenting, fitness, skill acquisition, trauma survival.

- **What types of services or products do you already enjoy giving to friends for free?** Examples could include baking, counselling, practical help, dog walking.

- **What skills/knowledge do you have a passion to continue to learn and develop?** For example: DIY, leadership skills, design, child care.

Really spend some time going through these questions. The more you think and analyse your own preferences, experiences, skills and qualities, the more you will think of other possibilities that may not have been initially apparent. The qualities and skills that you possess, and that could contribute to a successful business, may be so normal to you that you no longer even notice them. They may be so familiar to you that you don't value them enough to realise that they could be extremely valuable in someone else's life.

If you are having problems thinking of enough answers then ask a good, honest friend to give you feedback.

Once you have a long list of answers, spend some time looking through the list asking yourself these questions:

- Which of these answers makes me feel most excited?
- Which could be valuable to someone who does not have this?
- What can you do, say or create that would add value to someone else's life? (This could be a physical product, practical service, financial gain, emotional support, aesthetic beauty or any other way.)
- What would you be happiest doing? What could you continue to do every day, and continue to enjoy, even if it gets stressful or hard?

It is essential, for the longevity of your business, that your business reflects and connects with your natural talents and skills.

For example, it is not wise to go into independent stock trade just because you heard others have made big money. You will end up miserable, frustrated and probably broke if this does not compliment your natural strengths. You are suited to independent stock trade if your skills lie in analytic thinking, mathematics skills and your personal interests already lie in global affairs and economic trends. These qualities and interests have positioned you to begin a business which relies on analysis, mathematical predictions and an understanding of global affairs and economics.

The key to creating a sustainable business is the ability to analyse your strengths as a person and create a business which enhances this. It needs to be something you love, that flows easily from you, so you can work with passion and stamina no matter what challenges lie ahead of you... and there will be challenges!

Building any business is not easy but if you build something that connects with your passions, unique strengths and personal attributes then it will still be fun. It will be exhilarating rather than draining, engaging rather than depressing and you will feel determined rather than defeated. These are the qualities that will sustain you. They will bring you the motivation you need to keep seeking God for solutions, enabling, opportunities and wisdom to flow in your business. It is this invitation you make to God that I believe will create miraculous momentum, open doors and enable you to enjoy the journey.

One of the main reasons many Christians will discount themselves and never explore their entrepreneurial potential, is that they underestimate their own abilities and what God is able to do through them. They may only see entrepreneurial 'business' in high-powered, city-dwelling, corporate minority terms. They do not see the myriad of creative entrepreneurial opportunities right in front of them. They do not consider that their own skills and abilities could be of commercial value to someone else. They under-value the investment God has made into them through their natural propensity, experiences and knowledge. There are many entrepreneurs throughout the world who have created wildly successful and profitable businesses through unconventional ideas, interests and skills. The only thing difference between these creative entrepreneurs and those who only ever dream, is the courage and determination to offer their ECP to the public and risk the possible rejection or failure.

As Christians, we should be the most courageous people of all because we have the support, enabling and miraculous power of the creator of the universe behind us. With our identity firmly rooted in our acceptance and future in Christ we have nothing to fear when it comes to rejection, failure or embarrassment. Have faith that God can use and multiply his investment in you for maximum reward. You only need the courage and determination to offer your abilities to others. The natural skills, interests and abilities that God has invested in you have the potential to create reward, no matter how uncommercial it may seem to you. There are many creative industries that have the potential for extremely successful self-employed businesses such as travel, design, parenting, fitness, fashion, health, motivation, baking, crafting, comedy, photography, social connection, current affairs, animal care, beauty, shopping and so many more. Each one of these creative industries, although not obviously commercial, contain numerous stories of extremely successful entrepreneurs and there is no reason why this could not be you too.

As Christians, we are not called to pursue wealth itself, but rather to pursue maximum reward for the investment that God has placed within us. This will look different in your life to how it will look in mine. We should not be trying to pursue a quick buck, seduced by the promise of instant riches but rather we are looking to increase our wellbeing, rest and financial stability so that we can be effective for God in every area of our lives. Even if you do not think you have a world-changing invention or the right personality or skills this does not mean that you can't succeed. There are ways to monetise, multiply and develop almost any business in any industry by increasing the commercial appeal of the ECP, networking, stream-lining the manufacturing and delivery processes and automating the business to a mass-accessibility level. This "scaling up" of your business can result in an income equal to that of many investors, but you will have achieved it through a business you connect with on a personal level.

The solution, therefore, is to stay true to yourself. Be aware of the investment that God has given you, what is in your hand right now? What can you do well? What knowledge have you gained through your previous work, study or hobbies? What experience has God given you that you can now turn into a service or product to enrich the lives of others?

Whatever God has given you, whatever finance, whatever talent, whatever experience— no matter how insignificant it may seem— holds the potential to be turned into an ECP that will add value to the lives of others as well as your own. God has given you all that you need to pursue a creative, entrepreneurial life, the question remains, will you acknowledge and step into this potential?

Determination will always succeed over talent alone.

Neither a skill, a talent or a great idea is enough to create a successful business, determination is the key. The key ingredient needed to create a successful business is the commitment to keep learning, keep trying and keep adapting ... and any one of us can do this! You do not need to possess extraordinary talent, but only extraordinary perseverance and through Christ, each of us have the potential for this.

Market Research

Once you have your idea, the next important question to answer is whether or not this idea has the potential for profit. What seems like a good idea to you may not be a good idea to your potential customers! You need to know that someone will want to buy your ECP, or you do not have a viable business idea.

Before you waste any time on developing your product, you must, must, must do your market research because you need to know that there is potential for profit. If not, then this is going to become a very expensive experiment.

The best way to do market research is to research the alternatives. What comparable ECPs are already out there? They may not be exactly the same but there will be something similar.

Now write down:

- How much are they charging and how much profit would this price leave you after all your expenses (don't forget your full-time salary in this calculation too!)?

- What kind of clients do they appear to be attracting? What colours, style and branding are they using? What kind of person would this ECP appeal to?

- How popular are they? Check out their social media accounts to see how many people follow and interact with them? Can you see how many sales they have made? Do they have Facebook pages for paying customers only, how many people are in there?

- Look through their testimonials, what kind of people are they? How old are they? Where do they live? What do they value most about this ECP?

- Google it. Type your idea into Google and see what paid adverts pop up. If others consider this industry valuable enough to invest in with paid advertising then this is a good indication that there is money to be made.

- Do they have paid adverts on their website? If they have other companies advertising on their website then this is a sign that their product is not particularly commercial but sponsorship is their main income. This is not a bad thing and can be very profitable, it is just a different business set-up.

Once you have established that there is a current market and demand and, therefore, you have the potential for success, the next step is to create a business plan.

A business plan is not as scary as it sounds, it is simply a way of mapping out the predicted future for your business. What exactly will you sell, who exactly will buy it, what is your profit margin and how can you be sure of success. Traditionally a business plan was used to secure a loan from the bank, it was the analytical review of your new business idea that would persuade the bank that this was a safe opportunity for investment.
You may not need a loan (and I recommend that you don't, if at all possible) but creating a business plan can help illuminate whether or not this new business idea is a safe option for your own time and financial investment.

Head over to **www.businessofblessing.com** to get the Business of Blessing study guide, as this includes a 12 page Business Plan template, to make this exercise easy to complete.

Chapter 4

<u>The Nine Value Triggers</u>

Creating an Irresistible Product

"Tat" is a word that makes a regular appearance in our house.
I love budget homeware stores, I can't help myself. There is
something addictively satisfying about buying seven items for
the same price it would cost to buy one in another store. I am a
bargain hunter extraordinaire... I am my father's daughter!
The only problem is that what I consider to be value for money,
my husband Matt often considers to be cheap "tat".
One such day I was attempting to quietly sneak into the house,
arms laden with my bargain treasures and knick-knacks, when
he caught me red-handed in the hall. He laughed at my
expression, as guilty as a child caught with chocolate round
their mouth, and teased, *"Have you been out buying "tat"
again?"*
Matt is more concerned with quality than quantity. To him,
"value for money" is about enjoying the finer things, not settling
for mediocre in order to save a few pennies. This crosses over
into many other aspects of our lives... food, for example. Matt

likes expensive, quality food, but I am all about quantity, give me a budget buffet over a gourmet restaurant any day!

I am always fascinated that Matt can taste subtleties in food that seems absolutely fine to me. I always thought he was just fussy until one day when I was tucking into a delicious restaurant cheese board. I was three mouthfuls in before I realised that I was not eating cheese but lumps of butter!!! (I thought it tasted extra creamy!)

I realised then that it wasn't Matt who was over-obsessed with good food, it was me who had underdeveloped taste buds!

You see, everyone has different priorities and perspectives and this determines what they perceive as 'value-for-money'. The vast majority of potential customers who see the price of my current photography business think it is far too expensive (and I have had many people tell me this over the years too) and yet many of my paying customers have told me how reasonable my price is and how surprised they are that I am not more expensive. How is that possible? How can I be too expensive for some people and yet considered to be excellent 'value-for-money' by others?

It is because 'value-for-money' does not rest in the actual amount but in the value system that your customer holds. Value-for-money looks different from person to person because everyone has different taste, experience and expectations. Successful business is about creating a product that appeals to the taste buds of your ideal client and gets them excited.

Creating a successful and sustainable business is not simply about creating a fantastic ECP... you need someone to buy it! You need to create an ECP that is so desirable that enough people will pay you enough money to create a life-sustaining income from it. This is whole different ball game!

As we have already touched on, as a forward-thinking business owner, the question you are always asking yourself is, 'what can I offer that will add value to the lives of my customers?"

However, what a person is willing to spend their hard earned cash on varies wildly from person to person. One person may only buy second-hand clothing and cut their own hair but splurge on travel or craft materials or organic food. Another person may invest heavily in the decoration of their home and then rarely leave it whereas the next person lives in very modest housing but spurges on entertainment and their social life.

What we choose to spend our money on also varies dramatically depending on our season in life. It all hinges on the things that we, personally, value the most. Purchasing a product, service or experience, does not rest solely on how much money a person has but rather on the Value Triggers that they hold. One person has had a bad experience with a particular cheap product so now chooses to spend extra on better quality, while another is perfectly happy with the most basic option. One person can't stand the taste of cheap wine while another person can't taste the difference, and is quite happy with the cheapest bottle on offer. These Value Triggers are the things your customer personally values most in their lives, the things that they believe add more value to their lives than the money it costs to buy them. These are the possessions, experiences or connections that your customer can't live without.

The important thing to understand when building a successful business is that people will always find money for the things that are important to them. A successful business does not rest on finding clients with more money, but rather on locating and connecting with the Value Triggers that they already hold.

I have identified nine key Value-Adding Sales Triggers:

- **Creates more time.** This is any ECP which makes the life of the customer easier, less complicated, less pressured, less rushed or less difficult.

- **Improves well-being.** This is an ECP which promotes contentment, relaxation, motivation, mental and physical health, and wholeness.

- **Solves a problem.** This is an ECP which meets a practical need with a practical solution.

- **Provides measurable increase.** This is any ECP which provides an opportunity for increase in skill, opportunity, finance or efficiency.

- **Entertainment.** This is an ECP that entertains or engages intrigue, humour, amusement, imagination, distraction or escapism.

- **Connection.** This is an ECP which connects your customer with other people, with emotions, memories, opportunities, jobs or ideas.

- **Status.** This includes an ECP which provides an "exclusive club" feel; connecting a person with a perceived improvement in status through increased respect, acceptance or admiration of others.

- **Beauty.** This is any ECP that provides visual enjoyment or creative expression, such as jewellery, body art, photography, home design, art etc

- **Humanitarian**. This is an ECP that appeals to a person's sense of humanity and helps them feel that they are making a difference. These include social enterprises, social equity venture, fair trade or those with an eco-friendly element.

Every successful industry will have one, two or a combination of these Value-Adding Sales Triggers and these Value Triggers are the reason that customers will look for and purchase these ECPs. In a similar way, any business can increase their appeal and sales potential by adding a Value Trigger, or by communicating more clearly the Value Triggers they already possess .

Looking through these nine Value Triggers, can you see a way for your skills, experiences or qualities to add one or more of these values to the lives of those around you? This is the start of your ECP formation.

The most important factor to determining how successfully you will sell your ECP is your ability to communicate how your ECP meets one or more of these Value Triggers for your potential customer. If your product is not selling, it is either because you don't have a market or an audience (not enough people have heard about you) or you are not communicating your Value Triggers effectively enough. If nobody is buying from you it very rarely has anything to do with "changes in the market", being "undercut by cheaper businesses" but everything to do with the effective communication of your ECP's Value Triggers.

If your potential customer does not understand how your ECP will add value to their lives, in the areas that they care about, they are never going to give you their money.

It is never effective (or acceptable) to try to force, trick or manipulate your potential customer into buying from you. Using guilt, exaggeration or bad-mouthing your competition are, not only immoral selling techniques, they are also not the most effective. These are not God-honouring ways to sell any product. Equally, treating your potential client with indifference will be detrimental to your business success too. Customer indifference at a sales level comes in many forms but the main one is failing to communicate the Value Triggers provided by your ECP. Investing the time and effort to ensure that your potential client feels informed to make a good decision, will actually make it more likely that they will buy from you with confidence. God-honouring Sales is not about trying to coerce a potential client into buying but about empowering them to make the decision themselves. When they come to the decision for themselves they are more likely to buy quickly, and pay more, for your ECP.

I call this type of sales: Customer-Focused Sales.

This is because the customer's needs, emotions and values take pride of place throughout the entire sales process.

Let me try to illustrate how customer-focused sales can be so effective. I once contacted another photographer to book a photography training session. As I sent the email I told my husband, "I don't care how much she is charging, whatever it is, I will pay it." I was definitely her ideal client. I valued her knowledge and skill so much that I was willing to pay whatever she charged. I received this reply:

"I offer mentoring sessions at $500 per hour. Let me know. Cheers."

She was asking me to hand over $500 without any information or guarantees. Her reply offered no information, reassurance or any indication that that she cared about my needs.

I tried to get information but continued to receive short, clinical replies containing no information or reassurances. I had to walk away. What a shame, I had been so ready to buy!

It is possible that she did not want to come on too strong. She may have worried that by detailing exactly what we would cover— what her commitment as my coach was and what I would have learnt by at the end of the session— might come across as too pushy and "salesy". But her short, information-lacking emails actually had the exact opposite affect. It made me feel that she was only interested in my money with no motivation to add value to my life in exchange. She actually felt *less* trust-worthy. It made me want to run a mile because I had no idea what exactly I would be buying.

It was interesting that she is also a Christian who teaches business classes so this experience, from a potential customer point of view, opened my eyes to some basic mistakes that even christians, with the best intentions, can be making. And these mistakes are actually driving customers away.

If we are too scared to communicate the value of what we offer for fear of being too pushy or "salesy", we can actually push clients away. Customers WANT you to sell to them. Not the pressurised or coercing type of sales but the customer-focused kind. The kind that simply explains what the product is and how it can help, so that the potential customer can make an informed decision. The kind that acknowledges and supports their right to make their own choices, with all the relevant information.

By giving potential customers as much information as you can, anticipating their concerns, providing answers to their questions and describing the benefit and value of what you are offering, you are showing care for them as a person and upholding their human right to self-determination. Without the relevant information (and this includes the details of how your ECP can enrich their life) they can't truly make the best decision. By investing effort into communicating the details and benefits of your ECP you are reassuring your potential client that you understand that they deserve value for money. You are acknowledging their individual values, needs and desires, and communicating that you believe they deserve to be able to make the best decision for them. When you don't give a potential client all the information they need to make an informed decision you run the risk of them feeling belittled, undervalued and stripped of power. By actively 'selling' the details and value of your ECP, you are elevating your potential client and showing them respect and in my experience, they will respond to that.

By only focusing on the cost you are inadvertently giving the message that their money is the most important thing to you, not their happiness. This will always turn potential clients away. Of course, you need to state a price but your customer must understand that this is in the context of your commitment to provide them with value for money. You may have this commitment but have never thought to communicate it clearly to your customer before. I guarantee that the moment you begin to focus on communicating your commitment to your potential customer's Value Triggers, your sales will significantly increase because customers respond when they feel valued and appreciated.

Chapter 5

<u>Buyer Psychology</u>

The Art of Attracting Higher Paying Customers

Many years ago I was a full-time singer in a youth outreach hip hop band (which is hilarious if you know me because I am the least 'hip hop' person you've ever seen in your life!)

We would spend a week at a time in each school we visited, leading Religious Education classes to communicate our faith in Jesus and also teaching practical workshops in hip hop skills, dance and music. The week would culminate in an after-school concert. Following the mildly celebrious status we would gain with the kids over the week these concerts would always be bursting with hundreds of young people, waving their glow-sticks and cheering at the top of their lungs. I even remember one concert when the sheer volume of young people surging against the doors broke the mechanisms and we had to cancel the concert because nobody could get in!

With this in mind, let me tell you about one hilariously different concert. We always partnered with local churches and youth groups so that any young person who made a commitment to Jesus had instant connection to a local church. This one particular youth group were insistent that we held the after-school concert at their church building and not at the school. Despite several attempts to explain that the young people would not come to a building that they did not know, they would not be swayed and we eventually conceded to perform the concert at the church.

The day of the concert arrived and to say that the concert was a flop would be an understatement!

As I nervously peered around the curtains from back stage I didn't see the usual hoards of excited teenagers but three... yes, you read that right, just three young people, sitting in an empty hall.

The start time arrived and, in true professional manner, we set about performing our hearts out, with the same energy we would have given to thousands of people in an arena. However, beneath the surface, my brain was working overtime trying to think of a solution for the upcoming audience participation game— we needed three volunteers.

That was our entire audience!

Fortunately, in the hour before the participation game, three more young people arrived so we were able to have three volunteers whilst still leaving three audience members! To this day, this story remains one of the funniest concerts we ever performed (there was one that was even funnier but that will have to be a story for another time).

The problem boiled down to a lack of understanding of human psychology. You can have the best idea and polish it to perfection but if you do not understand human psychology, nobody will turn up. This is exactly the same for business; we must understand buyer psychology. You can have the best product available, and develop it to perfection, but if you do not understand buyer psychology, nobody will buy it! A good product alone is not enough to create sales.

This is one of the most common mistake new businesses make. They create a brilliant product and present it to the world and then are baffled by the tumbleweed silence. What did they do wrong? Why is nobody buying?

They then invest in further development of their product, wrongly assuming that the problem must lie with the product. When the business still refuses to take off they walk away dejected and confused, wondering why the world did not flock to buy their perfect product.

It is all about buyer psychology— understanding what makes a person want to buy anything. This is a huge topic and we are only scratching the surface but let's look at eight easy ways to use buyer psychology to start attracting higher-paying clients.

1

'Need' engages intellect, 'Want' engages impulse

Multimillionaire Zig Ziglar tells a fascinating story from the time that he was a door-to-door salesman. His company sold superior cooking pots and on this particular day he was in the home of an elderly couple who had no adequate cooking sets at all. They really needed these new pots and Zig knew it. He spent two hours doing all he could to highlight the couple's need and explain the solution that his product could provide. Alas, despite Zig's best efforts and the couple's obvious needs, they would not budge on their insistence that the pots were too expensive and they didn't have the money. Disheartened and more than a little confused Zig finally packed up and prepared to leave the house. As he was leaving he mentioned china and the elderly lady's eye's lit up. "China?" She said excitedly, "Do you sell china?"

Moments later, Zig left with a china order worth far more than the entire range of cookware!

How was that possible?

The couple had insisted they didn't have the money for something that they desperately needed and yet they miraculously produced that same money, and more, to buy a luxury they merely wanted. They were more than ready, at a moment's notice, to spend money on a decorative item over a practical item that they needed, simply because they wanted it. Herein lies a fundamental secret guaranteed to increase sales of any item in any industry: **Customers buy what they want not just what they need.**

Present a person with something they *need* and they will consider it, present a person with something they *want* and they will buy it.

'Needs' make a customer think logically, 'wants' make them think impulsively.

If you connect with your potential clients needs they will listen but they will cautiously evaluate their options. They will consider the pros and cons, they will shop around, try to find cheaper alternatives, consider how they can make do without it or try to create a DIY solution. The "need drive" causes potential customers to get practical and rational.

The "want drive" is far more powerful when it comes to spending money. When a person wants something they will do all the hard work of justifying the spend to themselves. They will convince *themselves* that your ECP is something they must have. They will give *themselves* reasons to purchase. They will literally bite your hand off to buy the thing that you are selling, because they want it.

'Wants' often grow out of 'needs' too. They are intrinsically linked. As we discover our 'needs' we often form our 'wants'. It is a combination of both 'wants' and 'needs' that drive our decision making process.

'Needs' relate to practical realities, 'wants' relate to emotional desires. 'Needs' are driven by the practicalities of today, 'wants' are driven by the emotional desires of tomorrow.

All decision making is driven by 'wants' and 'needs'. If we find a product that both meets our 'needs' and our 'wants' (both meeting our needs for today and our desires for the future), this is when we get excited. This is when we know we have found exactly what we're looking for and can't wait to hand over our money. If you can connect with both the 'wants' and 'needs' for your potential customer, your business is guaranteed to be a success.

2

Sell Benefits not Features

One of the most commonly committed selling mistakes is to sell features not benefits. A feature describes the physical attributes of a product, but a benefit describes the reasons to purchase.

A feature describes the process, a benefit describes the end result. And this is what your potential customer is buying: an end result.

Nobody wants a process, that involves work. People want a transformation. Your potential customer is looking to buy a better life. It is your job, when presenting your product, to communicate the end result, paint the mental picture, how will this ECP benefit or improve their life?

For example: Matt and I recently bought a new smoothie maker. It has 900 watt power... what does that even mean? Is that good? Is that bad?

I had no frame of reference because I had never bought a smoothie maker before so that number meant nothing to me.

900 watt power is a feature. It describes a measurable attribute, but that is not enough. I needed to know why I should want a 900 watt power smoothie maker. This is where the benefits come in.

What is the benefit of 900 watt power? The benefit is that it blends the smoothie faster. Now I can begin to understand why this feature will benefit me.

But we can also go one step further, what is the benefit of the benefit? The benefit of speedier blending is that it saves time in the morning. No rushing, no missing the bus, more free time, a few extra minutes in bed, less stress... the list goes on.

Once you start to explore the benefits of the benefits, the sky becomes the limit. Suddenly your potential customer can join the dots and see how one small, seemingly insignificant, feature can actually have a knock-on effect in their life in many positive ways. It is these effects that will convince a potential customer that they need to have your ECP in their life.

3
Purchasing Reflects Justification not Budget

It doesn't matter how much money your potential customer has, it is their justification of a product's value that determines whether or not they will purchase, not just their physical budget. I have had many business owners say to me over the years, "I just need to find clients with more money." This is actually one of the biggest mistakes for a new businesses to fall into:

assuming that their lack of sales means that they are not accessing a rich-enough clientele. This is a complete fallacy and can actually be causing you to attract 'deal-seeking' clients. Let me explain.

Even the world's richest, most elite customer base are not stupid. Nobody wants to spend more than they have to. Even the super rich know how to get maximum value for money and this is likely to be one of the reasons they are wealthy in the first place. They certainly didn't get rich by throwing their money away or over-paying where they did not need to.

No, the solution is not finding high-*earning* clients, but attracting higher-*paying* clients. This is a very different thing.

You see, everybody has the money for the things they value most. Their readiness to purchase does not rest solely on their disposable income but on their ability to justify the purchase.

Your potential customer could have the biggest bank balance in the world but if they can't justify the expense they will not purchase. Equally, a person on a very limited budget will still purchase if they can justify the cost.

It is our job to help potential customers to justify the cost of our ECP; to have an excuse to purchase. Why is your product a good investment?

We need to communicate the value of our ECP so clearly that a potential customer can easily justify the cost.

As soon as the value of a product appears more valuable than the money it will take to get it, this is when we buy. If your customer understands that they will get more value from your ECP than the money they'll lose, it becomes a no-brainer! It makes sense. It's like 'trading up'– you receive more value in real terms than the money you offered in exchange.

4
Preemptive Incentive

It is human psychology to be risk-averse. It is this fear of risk that keeps us alive on a wild planet, but this primal, survival instinct can affect your potential clients when faced with the prospect of parting with their money.

They have never bought from you before. They may have never even bought an ECP like this before and they will naturally start to look for all the possible risk factors. They are looking for the warning signs. They are looking for reasons NOT to purchase.

This is a fundamental principle that will utterly transform your sales process if you let it. When looking to sell (communicate) the value of your ECP, you must first stop and think through every possible reason that a person would have for NOT buying.

What possible reasons could a person give themselves to NOT take the risk and part with their money? These potential fears can then form the framework for your entire sales process. Everything you say, every illustration you give, every piece of information that you offer is designed to reassure these fears before they are even spoken.

I call this "Preemptive Incentive" because you are preemptively providing reassurance for any possible concerns or objections. It is when every single one of your potential customer's fears have been completely reassured that they will feel confident to purchase.

I promised earlier that I would tell you my secret advertising tactic that caused my singing lesson business to grow faster than other coaches in the area, despite charging twice as much.

I was teaching from home, in my slippers, from a very average flat in a very average neighbourhood. Yet customers were flocking, so much so that I quickly became permanently fully booked with over 100 people on a waiting list. How did that happen?

Well, first of all, I knew I had a great product and I knew who my target market was. I had invested a huge amount of time into developing my skills as a competent teacher and had done my 'product testing' (I had taught test clients who had all experienced improvement) so I knew that my product was genuine and valuable. I knew it would sell itself but how could I get people through the door? How could I get a new client to trust me enough to try it?

I decided to put my money where my mouth was and I offered something unheard of in the music tuition industry. I have never seen anyone offer this before and I have never seen anyone offer it since!

I offered a money back guarantee: *"See improvement in your first lesson or your money back!"*

This one simple tag line transformed the way my new business was perceived. I had several clients say that they took one look at my money-back guarantee and decided there and then that it was me or nobody. They trusted me instantaneously. That one line communicated more in 3 seconds, than pages of sales copy and testimonials. What those few words were actually saying was, *"You will learn far more with me than with any other teacher. No one else is offering this guarantee because you will not progress this fast with anyone else. I am going to save you money in the long run and help you achieve your goals quicker. You do not need to look anywhere else, these are the best vocal lessons available."*

That's a big message for a short sentence and it worked. In one sentence I had completely eliminated the risk to my potential customer. Psychologically they felt that they were getting a free lesson... but in reality, I was still getting paid!

It is important to stress at this point that this was a calculated risk on my part. This only works in an industry where the first payment is only the start of the professional relationship. I structured the first lesson to essentially be a sales pitch—establishing their needs, exciting them with the solution I could provide and leaving them with no doubt that future lessons were a must.

Once someone has received a final product there is absolutely no incentive for the unscrupulous customer to not turn around and demand a refund, for no reason, because they no longer need your service. This kind of advertising angle only works when there is the need for an ongoing business relationship so it is not in your customer's interests to abuse your offer.

Money back guarantees are also, not the only way to entice a sale, there are many ways of making a potential customer feel confident to purchase for the first time. It is about addressing your potential customer's fears and reassuring them of the quality and value they will receive. It is about leading the customer to a place where they feel it is riskier to *not* purchase, or that they will be missing out if they don't. It is about building confidence in both your product and your service. It is about removing the mental obstacles to a sale, anticipating their fears and objections and providing the education or reassurance preemptively.

This is Preemptive Incentive.

No-One Cares About You.

I know this sounds harsh but it is important to remember that, from a business point of view, your potential customer doesn't care about you outside of your role in their purchase. In the moment that they are investigating what you have to offer, they only care about themselves and how your ECP benefits them, and this is totally reasonable. You are about to ask them to part with their hard-earned money, it is natural for them to be asking the question: "*What's in it for me?*"

Think about when you last went to a supermarket, what occupied your thoughts most? Were you thinking about the history the shop, the dreams of the CEO or the lives of the employees serving you? Or were you thinking about your shopping list and how much each item was going to cost you?

Of course, in that moment, you were thinking about yourself: your needs, your schedule and your budget. This is reasonable and natural, and this is exactly the mindset that a potential customer will have when encountering your business.

Your potential customer is busy, they have things to do and a limited attention span. Your sales process needs to be all about the customer and their needs. I know on the surface this sounds obvious but you would not believe the number of business owners who actually, unknowingly, make their sales process about themselves and not their client. The important thing is not why you created this ECP but why you created this ECP *for them*.

Do not be tempted to talk about yourself, your dreams, goals and desires unless they are directly related to the service your customer will receive.

Your potential customers are not philanthropists, they are not going to give you money to support your dreams, maintain your lifestyle, fund your hobbies or create purpose for your life. Your message must be very clear, right from the start, that your business exists for your customer's happiness. Limit non-relevant information to one or two amusing personal facts and keep the rest of your story relevant to the needs or concerns of your customer. They do not care who you are outside your work, they care about why they should trust you as a professional, and ultimately, why they should choose your business over other alternatives.

6
Experience Beats Product

Ultimately experiences sell far better than products alone. This is why every aftershave advert you'll ever see will go something like this:

< Opening scene: Super hunky, shirtless man with arms the size of his legs, picks up his supermodel girlfriend on a ridiculously powerful motorbike and drives off into a tornado, coming out the other side with his hair still in a perfect quiff and getting a well-earned snog from the aforementioned girlfriend. >

They are selling an experience: 'If you wear this aftershave you will feel as good as this man'. You will feel as confident and as dashing, and you will gain the admiration of everyone around you. Imagine if an aftershave advert was simply someone holding up the bottle and saying, "Mmm, it smells really nice... like berries... with a hint of cinnamon."

I can tell you right now that the sales of the cinnamon aftershave will be far, far less that the sexy, tornado, motorbike man. We are all looking for experiences. We buy experiences not products, and your potential client is no different.

This buyer psychology principle is relevant for both product-based and service-based ECPs. You are not just selling a physical product but you are also selling an outstanding experience and a lifestyle transformation. This needs to be part of your sales process.

When a customer hires you directly, your personality becomes the main factor in the experience they will have. There is absolutely nobody else out there who has the same personality, experiences, motivations and humour as you. You are offering a one-of-a-kind experience. Your potential customer simply cannot buy this exact service anywhere else because there is only one of you. You need to sell this fact.

Be careful to keep your descriptions and focus to your professional personality— what makes you the best person to serve your customers needs? Keep your facts and stories relevant to your customer's need. Remember that everything you say must be designed to sell the benefits of spending with you and you alone. Your aim is that your potential customer feels more confident and inclined to purchase from you.

This also does not just mean simply saying: "I am unique and I am offering a unique service," ... if only life was that simple!

No, you need to be clever, descriptive and creative. What exactly makes you unique? How do you create a unique service that nobody else can emulate? You need to help a prospective customer to picture what it would be like to hire you over someone else. They need to be able to imagine the experience they are going to have. Be descriptive, be emotive and use key trigger words that are going to connect with your potential customer's desires as well as their needs.

You are not just selling a product or service, you are selling an end result, and this result will have a lasting effect on the rest of your customer's life. What is that result? How will their life be changed, for the better?

It is this experience, journey and transformation that will sell your ECP far more than facts alone, so make sure that this forms the main focus of your sales and marketing.

7
Nobody Bets on the Underdog

I have vivid memories from my student nurse training days— suddenly finding myself behind a curtain, with a vulnerable and terrified patient, trying to inspire total confidence in my extremely limited abilities to perform a routine task. On one occasion I was with an elderly gentleman and needed to perform an extremely intimate procedure. I have always been aware that I look much younger than I am so to this elderly gentleman I must have looked little older than a child!

He looked at me with fear in his eyes and asked, "*Have you done this before?*" "*Oh yes!*" I said with a dazzling smile and what I hoped was an infectious confidence. My positivity seemed to reassure him and he visibly exhaled, relaxed and allowed me to proceed. What I neglected to disclose was that I had actually only done this procedure once before and that was under supervision... I was literally shaking under my skin! I did NOT know if I could do this... but the reality was, I had to. For this patient's sake, I had to do this.

When you run your own business, every day is like being behind the curtain with that elderly patient. Every day is about portraying the confidence you do not feel and selling the abilities you only half believe you have.

The reality is this: nobody bets on the underdog, especially when it comes to business. Do not be tempted to go for the sympathy vote. Trying to persuade customers to buy from you because you are a small business or because you have bills to pay is not an effective advertising strategy. You are not a charity looking for handouts, you are a professional business offering a professional product or service. This is the only way to achieve the kind of prices you need to make your business viable and sustainable.

Similarly, don't down-play your product or abilities because you are new in business. Your potential customer does not need to know about your experience level or your fear level, only your professionalism and commitment to excellence. If I had let that elderly patient know I was scared, he would have immediately asked to see another nurse and I would have not have gained the valuable experience I needed to be able to help future patients.

I'm not saying you should lie but, equally, somethings don't need to be said unless it is to a good friend. If you even give a hint of inexperience, fear or desperation, your potential customer is going to run a mile and you will not gain the valuable experience (and income) that you need to make this business better. Parting with their money is always a risk for a potential customer so if there is any doubt in their mind that you or your ECP are not up to the task, they will immediately seek out an alternative.

Imagine that every sentence on your website, every advertisement on social media and every point of contact with a potential customer is like a job interview. You are selling yourself even if you do not fully believe in yourself. You need to make sure that you sound like the best candidate for the job.

It does not matter how you feel, only how your potential customer feels. Do they trust you? Do they believe in you? Are they excited about what you are offering? Do they feel compelled to choose you over other, potentially more qualified, options?

The reality is that you are better than you think you are. Passion and diligence counts for way more than experience and reputation alone. You are an expert if you know more than the person you are speaking to. You are trustworthy if you intend to do the best job that you can and ensure your customer's happiness.

When advertising your business you need to sell yourself. Speak as if you are better than you think you are. Speak as if you are more established than you are.

Imagine a day when your business is established and thriving, how will you speak about yourself then? How would you sell yourself then?

Start speaking like that now!

For your potential customer, this will create confidence that your business is professional and trustworthy. You may be scared witless but, as far as your website, social media and customer communication is concerned, business is great! It's never been better! Everyday is a good day. You are confident, you are experienced, you are professional and you are in-demand. When you communicate all the very best possible attributes of your business – perpetually describing your business on a good day – you will not only gain your potential customer's trust but also their custom.

Simple Wins the Race

And finally, keep it simple. Too much choice, complicated pricing options and over-explanation will scare potential customers away. Buying from you becomes too much like hard work and they will find an easier alternative. Make it as easy as possible for a potential customer to get the information they need, understand the pricing options and purchase your ECP.

Always look for the quickest way to say anything that you need to say.

Resist the urge to have more than three pricing options. Three pricing options is perfectly adequate to cover the range of choice. Your potential customer can ask for a customisation if they need it, but most will not need this.

Make the navigation on your website clear and instinctive, and make the contact options clear.

More words and more pricing options will NOT win you more sales. It is not a competition to see who can bombard a potential client with the most amount of waffle and choice.

Be the easy option; the path of least resistance. When you make it easy for your customer you are sparing them brainpower, essentially doing the hard work of making a decision for them, and this will make you the most appealing option.

Simple really does win the race... or in this case, the sale.

Chapter 6

<u>Customer-Focused Sales</u>

The Biblical Principle that can Increase Sales by 75%

I know what you are thinking— many people hate the idea of doing face-to-face sales. The word 'Sales' conjures up images of sleazy, dishonest, second-hand car salesmen or pushy door-to-door salesmen and I understand why. It did for me too!

The word "sale" itself comes from the old Proto-Germanic word "sala" or "sal" which means "to grasp or take", and also has linguistic connections to "hiding", "stealing", "theft", "concealing" or "keeping secret".

All of these are dishonest, corrupt and self-centred words. Is this really what 'sales' is— the art of stealing from another person?

This is not what God-honouring sales is about. In fact, this is not what any sales process should be about. Even in a business we are not exempt from the Biblical requirement to place the needs of others before our own.

"...value others above yourself, not looking to your own interests but each of you to the interests of others."
Philippians 2:3-4

86

True 'sales' — the God-honouring kind — is simply about connecting the right client with the right product for them. It is about giving, not taking. Empowering, not coercing. Giving your customer information, opportunity, freedom of choice and value. You can do that, right? That doesn't seem so scary, does it?

At the tender age of 18, I was fresh out of high school and about to embark on my first full-time working position in the big, wide world. I had a position as a telesales representative selling car insurance. I was beside myself with excitement for my first experience of working in an office! I bought my first pair of sensible, black court shoes, a below-the-knee pencil skirt and dark blue blouse. I walked down to my local train station in a sea of other commuters, to travel to the next town for my new office job. I felt so very grown up and so... corporate!
I was clip-clopping my way into adulthood.
Little did I know that my day was not going to be quite the triumph of sophistication I was dreaming it would be.
All the way to the train station I could feel that my heels were slightly sore although I decided to ignore it and continued to enjoy the exhilarating first leg of my new commute to work. By the time I reached the station however, it was very clear that my new plastic shoes and my baby soft skin were not a good mix! I had blood literally pouring from both heels where they had been rubbed raw in the ten minute walk. The inside of my precious new black court shoes were equally stained dark red.
I didn't even have any tissues so I was forced to resist the urge to die of embarrassment as I continued to drip blood onto the revoltingly dirty train floor (which I was now standing on barefoot).

The kind lady opposite me took pity and gave me a tissue with which I spent the fifteen minute commute trying to staunch the flow of blood, but it still kept coming!

As I reached my stop, I desperately tried to put my 'office shoes' back on but the pain was crippling. Therefore, I made the depressingly unsophisticated decision to carry my new shoes and walk barefoot up the streets, in full view of a hundred of my new colleagues. I trailed blood all along the pavement and up into my new office block. I slipped into the main reception as discretely as I could and uttered the very first words of an adult working life that would span the next 45 years: "Do you have a plaster please?"

How desperately unglamorous!

But, despite such an unromantic start to my adult working life I am so grateful that my first position was in such a historically high-pressured sales environment. I saw for myself, the under-hand tactics used to squeeze every last sale. I was under pressure by my manager, my supervisor and my co-workers to use dishonest and coercive techniques to trick, scare or pressure a potential customer into a sale. I was encouraged to steal sales from other workers and was reprimanded when I didn't. With a commission-based bonus system, making a sale was the most important goal in the mind of all my colleagues.

I remember praying and crying out to God saying, "There must be another way! There must be a way that I can be faithful to my duty in my job without lying, stealing or compromising the conscience you have given me?"

I was determined to try and allow my calling to love others to override my desire for self-gain. Oh, I wanted the commission of course, don't get my wrong! I am not THAT hyper-spiritual! But, I was not prepared to get it at the expense of someone else.

I refused to try to persuade a customer to buy when I could see that it was not the best product for them. I refused to steal sales from my co-workers and I refused to use any of the expected "sales" tactics to pressurise, scare or trick potential customers into a sale.

Everyday I prayed that God would show me that He could be trusted to reward my efforts to honour him and the customers I was serving. I prayed for sales; I put a figure on it each morning. I took the pressure of success out of my own hands, off of my potential customer, and placed it firmly in God's hands. I decided to believe that my potential customer did not hold the key to my provision, God did. I would not look at a potential sale as the solution to my need, I would look to God. I brought my need before Him and decided to trust him for the results rather than try to fight to make it happen in my own strength.

I began to pray, every single day— on my previously disastrous commute— that God would allow me to be an example of another way. Another way to sell, another way to be profitable, another way to be successful... and he did.

When I think back, it still blows me away even now... God's way really does work!

Every day I was earning four to five times higher than anyone else on my team. I was one of the highest sellers on my floor (around 200 people) and I even met several colleagues from other floors who said, "Sarah-Jane? Aren't you that girl on the second floor who sells all those policies?"

I had gained a reputation throughout the company as one of the most successful sales reps and yet I was refusing to utilise any of the usual dishonest "sales" practices.

I remember being reprimanded by a colleague when he overheard me refuse to steal a sale from another worker. I remember pointing to the sales board (which clearly showed my twenty sales compared to the two or three of every other team member) and said with a smile, "Look, whatever I'm doing it's clearly working so just let me do my thing!"

I did not fully realise it then, but I was practicing something that I have now termed, "Customer-Focused Sales".
And it worked!
I learnt in those early months that success does not need to be at the expense of others. No demand from management or colleagues ever outranks the command that I have already received from God. And I learnt, most importantly, that God can be trusted to honour and reward honesty, diligence and self-sacrifice.

I have seen this same uncharacteristic success in each one of my businesses and it is too consistent to be a coincidence. I honestly believe that a daily refocus on God as my provider and a dedication to treating others as I would want to be treated, has invited the blessing of God into my work. The principle is clear, God can be trusted to honour and provide for us when we live in obedience.
Customer-focused sales, first and foremost, represents the commitment to place the needs of the customer above your own. This is the God-honouring approach to sales and will invite God's blessing onto your business.

"Put yourself aside, and help others get ahead.
Don't be obsessed with getting your own advantage."
Philippians 2:3 (MSG)

Customer-focused sales is so successful because it is built on trust. Your potential customer is not stupid, they can tell if your primary focus is what you can get from them and they will run a mile! This is why the Bible says:

"Love from the centre of who you are, don't fake it."
Romans 12:10 (MSG)

This doesn't just relate to greed either, this can just as easily happen through desperation too. Money is tight, bills are mounting and a potential customer suddenly appears... it is too easy to have dollar signs ping up in your eyes and begin to see a potential client as a commodity rather than a person.
Not through any callousness of heart, but through a misunderstanding of who your provider is. You do not need this sale... no, you really don't!
You may argue: "Yes, but this sale could solve my financial problems this month! This sale could pay for X, Y or Z."
The problem with this is that you are placing your hope in your potential customer not God. You are placing your future, your security, your happiness in whether or not they buy, and there is no joy to be found in a life like this:

"This is what the Lord says:
Cursed is the one who trusts in man,
who draws strength from mere flesh
and whose heart turns away from the Lord.
That person will be like a bush in the wastelands;
they will not see prosperity when it comes.
They will dwell in the parched places of the desert,
in a salt land where no one lives.

But blessed is the one who trusts in the Lord,

whose confidence is in him.
They will be like a tree planted by the water
that sends out its roots by the stream.
It does not fear when heat comes;
its leaves are always green.
It has no worries in a year of drought
and never fails to bear fruit."
Jeremiah 17:5-8

If you can fully grasp this principle it will transform your business, I promise. It totally transformed mine.

By focusing on your customers, or your lack of them, you are actually looking to man for your provision, relying on mere flesh to meet your needs. Without realising it, you are turning your heart away from God and this is why you will find yourself stressed, overworked, doubting, desperate and miserable. You will feel like you are living in a desert. You will not be able to see blessing or celebrate each sale and success when it comes because you are too busy mourning a previous loss or worrying about future ones.

If you are living in this desert place, you will find that any rejection in your business will send you spiralling into despair and wanting to give up. You are unknowingly focused on what you don't have rather than what you do have. You are being robbed of the joy of God's provision today because of thinking over the past disappointment or worrying about a future one. You are prevented from enjoying the blessings that are already in your hand.

The solution? Let this truth sink in: your customer is not your provider... God is. Your prospective customer's money is not the answer to your financial problems or business success, God is. Don't just say it, believe it, live it!

God is your provider, God is your sustainer, God is your security and God is your hope. God is your provider and He is willing and able to meet all your needs in a variety of amazingly creative ways.

My stress levels fell on a monumental scale the day I fully realised and accepted this truth. Not just as head knowledge, but as a core belief that effected everything I do, say and think. I consciously and vocally handed my business account books over to God. I said;

"Father... can you please be in charge of the money side of things from now on? I'm going to leave the figures up to you and trust you that the numbers will add up to the income that I need.

I'm going to get on with all the things I can do. I'll do my marketing, my advertising, my sales, networking and client communication and leave the results up to you.

I am going to celebrate every new prospective client, thanking you that they found me in the first place, and I'm going to leave it up to you whether they book or not.

I'm going to enjoy the challenges and encouragements of today, and leave the future to you."

I began to experience peace and joy in my business in a whole new way... and what's more amazing is that my business began to take off. My sales increased. To this day, I am still unsure whether things actually improved or whether my eyes were just opened to see my blessings. Either way, things just felt easier.

I experienced first-hand that the promise (and warning) in this scripture is true and tangible. Focus on your prospective sale and you will live a stressed, depressed and unsatisfying life. Focus on God as your creative and faithful provider and you will live in peace and overwhelming blessing, not only in your business, but in every area of your life.

One verse that used to really puzzle me, suddenly made perfect sense in the context of this lesson I had learned.

"Whoever has will be given more;
whoever does not have, even what they have
will be taken from them."
Mark 4:25

This always confused me because this message doesn't seem to make any sense in context of the rest of scripture which has a consistent message of provision for the poor... that is, until I read this verse in the context of attitude. I felt God saying:

"If you focus on what you have, rather than what you don't have, you invite my abundance, and will have the eyes to see and enjoy it... but if you focus on what you don't have, you will be blinded to blessing and will be unable to enjoy even what you do have."

Our attitude of heart affects the reality of the world around us. When we truly have God in his rightful place in our hearts as our provider— sovereign and loving— then we are released to enjoy blessing without fear or worry. Sales can then become about the most important things: giving to others, giving choice, giving information, giving opportunity and adding value to the lives of those who buy from us.

When your primary focus is your client's gain (giving them an outstanding service and a superior product) they will sense this and will trust you. Your sales will sky-rocket as a result.

For whoever wants to save their life will lose it,

but whoever loses their life for me will find it.
Matthew 16:25

So much of our spiritual life is an oxymoron; in order to gain life you must be prepared to lose it. The first will be last. It is no different with biblical business; in order to increase sales you must be prepared to lose them. But this comes with a promise, a continuing theme throughout scripture; sacrifice releases God's blessing.

Just as Christ's sacrifice released God's blessing, so our sacrifice releases God's abundance. When we give up our desire for self-gain we open our lives to receive God's gain instead. This may look different to what we imagined but it is always good.

So if you want (or desperately need) more sales in your business, instead of working non-stop— working yourself to the bone in an attempt to try to make it happen in your own strength— spend time your knees, thanking God that He already knows your needs and has promised to provide.

"Therefore I tell you, do not worry about your life, what you will
eat or drink; or about your body, what you will wear.
Is not life more than food, and the body more than clothes?
Look at the birds of the air;
they do not sow or reap or store away in barns,
and yet your heavenly Father feeds them.
Are you not much more valuable than they?
Can any one of you by worrying add a single hour to your life?

...So do not worry, saying, 'What shall we eat?' or 'What shall we
drink?' or 'What shall we wear?'
For the pagans run after all these things,

and your heavenly Father knows that you need them.
But seek first his kingdom and his righteousness, and all these things
will be given to you as well."
Matthew 6:25-27,31-33

God knows your needs. He knows which bills need paying and He knows what you need for a healthy, happy and restful life. Once we let go of the fear of losing a sale through our unshakeable faith in God's provision, we can begin to make the sales process about our client; what do they need and what do they value? What is the best product for them? What is the right choice for them? When we connect with the client's values and demonstrate a willingness to walk away if our ECP is not right for them, we will earn something far more valuable; their trust. And ultimately, if you can build a trustworthy business, you are very unlikely to ever be short of customers.

Chapter 7

Starting Out: Investment

How to Start a Business with No Capital

One of the hardest balancing acts in any new business is deciding where the line is between a wise and a reckless investment.

In my early days of business I found myself pondering multiple types of businesses and having a lightbulb moment: all successful business is built on risk! I thought back to my old boss when I was a singer, his entire business was built on risk. He would pay for a theatre for the night and then sell the tickets to the show. If he could not sell enough tickets to cover the cost of the venue, pay all his staff and expenses, cover his advertising costs and create profit then he would suffer the financial shortfall. Every single day was a risk for him but rather than shy away from the risk he looked it in the eye and said: "Bring it on! I accept the challenge."

All business takes risk, determination and sacrifice to build. There is no such thing as a risk-free business. The Oxford English Dictionary definition of an entrepreneur is someone who personally accepts the risk of starting a business in the hope of profit. This is what entrepreneurs, throughout all history have done, and you will be know different. Wisdom comes in knowing which risk to accept and how much to invest at each stage.

My husband Matt and I have a three questions we ask ourselves when facing big financial decisions in our business:

1) **"Can we afford it?"** Do we actually have the capital to cover this? Could we live without the money if we were to lose it?

2) **"Is there a cheaper option?"** Can we minimise the financial risk and test the waters on a smaller scale first? Can we get the ball rolling and beginning earning enough now to cover this bigger future expense?

3) **"Can we afford to live with the 'what if'?"** What if it worked? What if this was the thing that propelled our business forward? If we didn't try, would this questions haunt us: what if?

If you can live with this possible regret, or if the risks seems so great that you would actually prefer to live with the lost potential rather than live with the potential consequences, then the answer is definitely DO NOT do it!

You need to live in peace, and if you will find more peace in living with a 'what if' than the potential consequences, then this is unlikely to be the right move for you, in this season.

If, however, you can't live with the 'what if'— if you would spend your whole life frustrated, wondering if things could have been different— then this is a risk you can't afford to **not** take!

This is how you can always have peace. If your plan works, great, but equally, if it fails, you still have peace, knowing that you had to at least try. You will never regret taking the risk because you could not have lived with the knowledge that it might have worked.

We also know that, in God, nothing is wasted. Every experience produces lessons that God can use for good. Lessons are just as important as successes when building for the long term. We often learn so much from past failures, no matter how painful, because they provide clarity and wisdom for the future and, often save a lot of time, energy and heartache in the long run.

If you have the money to spend, and you decide that you can't live with the 'what if', and consciously and prayerfully accept the risk with conviction and determination, you create a focus of mind that invites God's peace.

> "You will keep in perfect peace those whose minds are steadfast, because they trust in you."
> **Isaiah 26:3**

A moving ship is much easier to steer than a stationary one. God needs us to move, to take action. He can open the door of opportunity but you need to push on it first. Test the waters. Ask yourself the question: "*What is in front of me right now? What opportunities do I have? What possibilities excite me? What ideas do I have? What value can I bring to my world?*"

When you ask these questions and a door of opportunity appears, it is your responsibility to push on it. It may be the right one or it may be the wrong one. The door may open or it may not, but you will never know unless you push it and this will take risk. It will mean financial, emotional and time investment without an assurance of return, but if you can't live with the "what if" then you must push that door and trust God for the outcome.

In the early days of our businesses, Matt and I were newly married. We were stone-broke from spending every penny of our meagre savings on our wedding. We even used our wedding gift money to pay back the family loan we had taken. Matt had only started his business recently and was in the industry's quiet season. He had no prospective income for months. We had already discussed how it would be almost impossible to both live off one income... and then I unexpectedly lost my long-term business contract... just 3 days after our wedding!

Without any warning, we were thrown into the terrifying position of being genuinely and utterly broke.

We sat together on our honeymoon, just days after our wedding and wrote down exactly how much money we needed for our home, basic living expenses and tax bills. It amounted to £2,000 a month and we had two weeks to find the first lot.

With no jobs or prospects of work, this looked like an impossibility but we were not worried. We knew that God holds us in the palm of his hand (Isaiah 49:16) and owns the cattle on a thousands hills (Psalm 50:10).

We laughed and said, "Well, I guess this is a good place to start a marriage from... the only way is up now!"

We prayed every single day, not for finance itself, but for the opportunity to work... and God provided. Sometimes through customers and sometimes through unexpected and miraculous financial provision.

We learned so much in those early days, not only about business and our own personal abilities and strength as a couple, but also about God's faithfulness and the importance of taking action to release God's provision. God cannot bless the work of your hands (Deuteronomy 28v12) if your hands are not doing anything. Your business will not advertise itself, industry connections will not magically appear and customers will not buy through an inefficient sales process.

Matt and I worked hard, really hard, doing the everything we could see to do and our businesses grew very quickly. But it was never easy. We were scammed, robbed and wasted thousands of pounds. We were betrayed, attacked and embarrassed. We bought tens of websites that never got used and spent countless hours investing in ideas that never took off.

But our attitude was that we weren't wasting time or money but rather that we were inviting opportunity. We were working with our hands, doing what we could see in front of us to do, knowing that God could and would bless the work of our hands if we just did something.

I remember thinking, "*Something has to work! We are so determined, trying so much harder, and taking so much more risk than many others. Surely one of these doors has to open one day*" ...and it did.

Through trial and error, sacrifice and sheer determination we created successful businesses for ourselves. We learned something different from each and every "failure". Each disappointing, embarrassing or expensive mistake only made our future businesses more successful.

Through it all, we had peace. We knew that God had the ability to create business through us if we were willing to put in the hard work and reject the fear of failure.

We are called to live lives of reckless faith but this does not mean being unwise. Investing in new business can more closely resemble gambling if it is done out of impatience, greed or carelessness. There are no shortcuts. You cannot avoid the process. You can't buy your way out of the learning curve.

"Those who work their land will have abundant food,
but those who chase fantasies have no sense."
Proverbs 12:11

When this verse was written, "working the land" was most people's business, it was how they made their money. It is good to work hard on your business— and to not be seduced by the promise of instant results— just like it was hard to work the land. 'Working the land' is not like my rosy childhood memories of picking strawberries (and eating most of them) on a balmy summer's evening. No, it would have been hard work and was a long-term effort with months of heavy, physical toil. Chasing, what looks like, an alternative to working hard is a fantasy. The struggle is good, the process is all part of the journey. It is how we grow, it is how we learn, it makes our business stronger.

Borrowing money out of impatience, to try to avoid the hardship of the process, will not only rob you of a crucial spiritual foundation for your business but also exponentially increases the financial risk you face and the stress you will experience.

"Wealth from get-rich-quick schemes quickly disappears;
wealth from hard work grows."
Proverbs 13:11 (NLT)

The key to wisdom with a new business investment is to ask yourself what motivates your investment. Are you trying to cut corners, get to the finish line quicker or wanting to look better in front of others? Are you too proud, impatient or perfectionist to start at the bottom and work your way up?

Is your plan for the long-term or short-term?

Investing in long-term gain is a biblical principle. Investing recklessly, with the promise of short-term riches, is gambling. As far as possible, start your business within your means.

"Don't gamble on the pot of gold at the end of the rainbow, hocking your house against a lucky chance. The time will come when you have to pay up; you'll be left with nothing but the shirt on your back."
Proverbs 22:26-27 (MSG)

Getting a business loan is not wrong if it is completely necessary, and especially if you can absolutely guarantee the repayments without any hint of doubt or potential for failure. I also understand that for some types of business a loan is unavoidable, however, I also see that many business loan situations could have been avoided if the borrower had been prepared to build more slower and with more caution. Being content to grow a business slowly, within your means, is a wise way to protect against financial disaster.

"...the borrower is the slave to the lender."
Proverbs 22v7

Biblical business is about make money your slave, not become a slave to money yourself. Funding a business within your own means helps protect your family from the risk of financial slavery. If your ideas fail to grow in the time scale you hoped, the worst-case scenario is that you may have to live frugally for a little while longer. Borrowing money is a slippery slope should things not work out quite as expected. The reality of losing your home, or worse, will significantly increased once loan repayments, bailiffs and court orders are involved.

> "The plans of the diligent lead to profit as surely as haste leads to poverty."
> **Proverbs 21:5**

My advice is to always start small, wherever possible. What is within your means right now? What could you afford to lose? Yes, we need to be brave, and to exercise reckless faith but this relates more to the emotional and physical hurdles of actually getting the ball rolling like writing a plan, building a prototype, connecting with other professionals, advertising yourself or creating physical targets. Any investment you make must be calculated and manageable. You must be sure, to the best of your ability, that you will be able to pay yourself back with even more profit.

> "Wealth gained hastily will dwindle,
> but whoever gathers little by little will increase it."
> **Proverbs 13:11 (ESV)**

When Matt first started his photography career, he was in a catch-22 situation. He needed a decent camera in order to charge a decent price, but he needed to charge a decent price in order to be able to afford a decent camera. What could he do?

He could have got a loan to get the best camera on the market but instead he opted to build from the ground up through hard work and determination. He bought a mediocre camera, it wasn't great but it did a good enough job to get him started. He kept his day job and took on test clients in his spare time, charging a small amount. As the income began to slowly trickle in, he was able to live off his job income and reinvest all his photography earnings back into his new business. It was not long before he was able to upgrade his camera in stages, increasing his price as he went, until he was able to replace his job earnings with his new photography earnings.

Even if you are currently in a high-earning job or have received a financial windfall, I would still advise to start small and working up, rather than throwing a large sum of money into something that may end up being a fad.

You see, you never know what God has planned or how exactly things will work out. What if your first business idea actually turns into something else? What if your target markets turns out to be an entirely different group of people? What if circumstances change and you have to move home or readjust your commitment level? If you invest too heavily in something that is still just an idea, you may end up investing too heavily in the wrong 'step'.

> "A man's heart plans his way, But the Lord directs his step."
> **Proverbs 16:9 (NKJV)**

God will direct the steps you need to take, to get you where you need to be, but they may look different to ones you expected!

Create a financial buffer. Have at least three months income in a separate savings account (separate to your regular savings). This is specifically allocated to cover your living expenses should you find yourself in difficulty in your new business.

Having a small emergency buffer will allow you to take your time— making wise decisions for the long-term health of your business, not hasty decisions motivated by short term desperation.

"Ants are creatures of little strength, yet they store up their food in the summer."
Proverbs 30:25

*"The prudent see danger and take refuge,
but the simple keep going and pay the penalty."*
Proverbs 27:12

It is wise and biblical to create a financial buffer. Create room for error and for unforeseen delays. We are urged in Proverbs to foresee 'dangers' (possible problems) and plan/find a refuge.

If I have learned anything, from my limited time on earth, it is that everything takes longer than we first imagined it will! Your business will be no different.

No matter what you've heard, building your business will take longer than you imagine. If you have the added pressure of financial strain, you will be tempted to panic, making impulsive decisions that may affect the long-term success of your business. You need to allow yourself freedom to operate from a position of strength, thinking rationally not emotionally, and not being tempted into pursuing wrong clients, connections or investments.

Often this means starting to build your business in your spare time first. Don't run out and quit your day job until you have a specific plan for your new business and have already got the wheels in motion to make it a reality.

Build slowly, replacing your income as you go. Reduce your hours as and when you can afford to, or when your ability to honour your work commitments to your boss or your new customers is compromised.

When I started my first singing teaching business I had the benefit of a two month notice period before the end of my contract. I began working evenings and weekends for those two months in order to create a new job to transition into at the end of my employment. It was hard, don't get me wrong, and ordinarily I am a passionate advocate for healthy work-life balance with plenty of rest... but sometimes you are faced with a short-term period where two seasons overlap and you just have to knuckle down and get through it. I worked hard for those two months knowing I was building for the long-term. I could see the upcoming 'danger' and was taking refuge. I was creating a new career for myself so that I could transition fairly easily out of my job and into my new business.

I also needed to test, in those two months, whether this was actually a bad idea. Was there even the market? Would anyone pay me for what I knew? Could I teach effectively and help my clients improve? Did it look possible to build a healthy enough income doing this? These were questions that I needed to answer but it would have been too late to finish my job and then find out that this was not the door God was opening.

This is another way to create a buffer, making time for trial and error, when you can still afford for it to fail.

If you find yourself unexpectedly and suddenly without a job or income for any reason then you must weigh up what is the most profitable use of your time. Job hunting and going for interviews is a time-consuming process. It may be that this time could actually be more profitably spent on your new business if you have a clear plan of action to follow. Again, you need to be wise and make the best decision for your family. Assess, critically and realistically, how quickly you could begin to create a profit with your business compared to how quickly you could find temporary employment. How actionable is your business plan or is it still just a vague idea? Also weigh up how easy it would be to invest time into your new business versus the challenges of starting and learning a new position as an employee. I am confident that with wisdom and prayer you will feel a peace about which path is the right one for you.

If you are living hand-to-mouth with no spare income, or worse still, going into debt every month, then this is not an ideal time to start a new business. First, focus on creating a financial buffer for your business. Being in that position is a great opportunity to begin creative budgeting. Make a list of every outgoing you have and begin to brainstorm which areas you can save money in. Most of us can find at least one way to creatively budget and create more margin in our finances. This added finance, however small, can give you the investment you need to get started.

Just like Matt did with his basic camera, start by investing in the bare essentials. What are the very basic things you need in order to test your idea? Start earning from your idea, even if it is just a small amount. This is the reassurance you need to trust that your business idea is a viable one. You can then begin to confidently reinvest your profits into improving your ECP and charging a higher price. This is how you can build from the ground up with wisdom and longevity.

Chapter 8

The Business Fire-Starters

The Essential Checklist to Launch a Successful Business

When we were first married, and without any jobs, savings or potential income, I began pushing every single door I could see in front of me. I had recently learned to make soap and they had been a big success with my friends. One friend had such sensitive skin that she couldn't use anything other than pure water. When she tried my soap, she was amazed. It was the first product she was able to use that didn't inflame her skin. I knew I had a great product, and I enjoyed making it.

I had a lot of leftover, handmade soaps from our wedding favours so I wondered about selling them. A friend invited me to share her stall at a local craft fair so that I could test my new soap-making business idea.

I thought to myself, "*If this works, then I'm going to make so many soaps... I'm going to make more soaps than you've ever seen in your life... I will be the soap queen!*"

The day of the fair arrived and I lovingly displayed my surplus soap collection on the stall.

I sold five.

Not exactly the rush I had hoped for!

But the thing I found most informative was watching the lady directly opposite who also had a soap stall. The only difference being... her soaps were amazing! They were bigger, more colourful, more creative and much cheaper than mine.

I knew in that moment that I could not compete.

Maybe if I had the luxury of time to build up experience and bulk production processes I could have, but Matt and I needed money, and we needed it fast! This was definitely not the way to get it.

And that was the end of my shortest career so far, as a professional soap maker.

It is crucial to understand the market you are going into, so you can gauge where you fit and whether this is a viable business. You need have the right research, pricing and processes to make sure that your business is the biggest success it can be, in the shortest time possible.

So make sure you have implemented these "Fire-Starters" to confirm if your new idea is viable and ensure that your business will grow as quickly as possible.

Market

With any commercial business you need a target market; an ideal client. Are there people out there who will want to buy what you are selling? Is there is a demand?

The first way to test any new ECP is to test the concept on your immediate community: your family, friends and colleagues. By test, I mean, do they value your product enough to actually pay full price for it?

The next stage is to share your prototype on social media, as this will connect you with people you don't know, and gauge the response again.

This is the really valuable market research stage.

Through social media, we have the unique opportunity to do what it would have previously taken a small army of researches with clipboards to do on a Saturday morning. At the click of a button, you have access to everyone you have ever known and everyone they know too. People from all walks of life. This is a phenomenal opportunity and a great way to gauge public response to your new idea.

Another valuable way to do market research, without even getting your hands dirty, is to see what is already out there. What are people already buying? Are there similar companies? Look at their branding (their colour pallet, images, wording etc). What does their customer base look like? How much are they charging? Do you have unique selling features? Can you compete on price? Can you compete with them on value or experience?

If you find that there is nobody currently in your industry, this does not necessarily mean that you have discovered an untapped market. It's possible that many have previously tried and failed so don't get too excited. Proceed with caution.

The best industries to enter are those that are already thriving. A thriving industry means that an increasing number of the general public are aware of their need and are already looking for a solution. Half of your work is already done! The challenge is finding a way to stand out from the crowd with a unique selling feature.

Market Edge

Next you need a market edge, a unique selling feature. If you can identify, and communicate, the unique features of your ECP then there is always 'room for one more' in any industry.

There is room for you, there is room for your business. You have the potential to rise to the top even in an over-saturated market.

For example, at the time of writing this book, my main business is international wedding photography. When Matt and I started in photography it looked impossible. Photography was, and still is, an oversaturated market. The sheer amount of choice and rock-bottom prices, meant we could have just given up before we even started.

We saw, however, that there were several photographers who appeared to be unaffected by the surge in low budget photography options. They were still charging high prices and attracting large volumes of luxury clients. This gave us the reassurance we needed, to know that success was possible even in an over-crowded industry. If they had made it then there was no reason why we couldn't too!

So, in an industry where thousands had failed before me, I started my photography business... and what do you think happened?

Within 6 months, I had a full-time income and within a year I had tripled my prices. Within two years I was photographing all over the world and within three years I was mentoring photography businesses internationally.

Why? Because, as with every other commercial product or service, success is only around 5% reliant on the product itself and 95% on how you present this product to the public.

Success does not lie in whether your product is brilliant but in whether or not a potential customer can understand _why_ it is brilliant. You need a unique advertising angle, a unique selling feature.

This is known as your market edge— the unique features that makes your business stand out from the crowd and get noticed.

Potential customers need to know how your ECP is different from any other similar product or service they could buy.

If you are struggling to know what your unique strengths are, the simplest solution is to compare yourself to your competition. How is your ECP different in appearance, experience, function or result? You are looking for the subtle differences that you have.

One of the most common mistakes for any new business, is to look at the competition and think, "Well, they are doing X, Y or Z... I will just do that too."

Aiming to replicate their exact business or advertising will never give the best results. Their customer base is already happy. They are already the king of their kingdom. You are never going to propel your business forward if you are always playing catch-up with your competition. This is a guaranteed way to be stuck bringing up the rear.

No, when you look at your competition you are not looking for the ways that you are similar, you are specifically looking for the ways in which you are different.

What makes you unique?

What are you offering that they don't?

What can you personally bring to the table that gives your business a different focus, experience or process?

How is your ECP designed to be different, to specifically serve needs of a specific group of people?

This is your unique selling feature, your market edge. Advertise this. Make a fuss about it, never stop talking about it. Ensure every sales conversation and all your website copy, focuses on these unique features.

If you copy the tag lines, descriptions or tactics of another business your message will get drowned out like white noise. When your uniqueness sings through your advertising, website and communication, you will create a buzz around your product. People will get excited. They will recognise that this is not a message they have heard before, and therefore, this is not an ECP they can buy anywhere else. You begin to attract customers who are set on buying from you, and you alone.

They will stop shopping around because they understand that, in your business, they have found exactly what they're looking for.

Profit

It's sounds obvious but your business must be designed to make profit. As a God-honouring Business of Blessing, we need create a business that offers value, we need to be placing the needs of our customers first and we need to guard against the love of money, but this doesn't mean creating an inefficient business incapable of generating significant profit.

There are three types of value-adding enterprise: philanthropy, charity and entrepreneurialism. It is really important to see where the line between each of these of lies.

Philanthropy is benefiting society at personal expense.
Charity is benefiting society at communal expense.
Entrepreneurialism is benefiting society at the user's expense.

Everything that benefits society, comes at a cost. No gain in life is ever free. Even the gospel itself, although free to the listener, comes at a great cost. There is always a cost involved with improving the lives of others.

Philanthropy pays for the cost itself, on behalf of the recipient— the money comes from a single individual.

Charity pays through a community— a collection of individuals and/or government bodies donating to cover the cost on behalf of the recipients.

In business, the recipient pays for the cost themselves.

Don't be embarrassed that your ECP comes with a cost, this is a normal part of life, there is always a cost to everything, whether we see it or not. The hard concept for Christians to grasp can be that this cost is more than just the basic functioning costs of your business. The cost includes your time, energy, creating a financial buffer, creating excess for further product development, providing for retirement, compensating for experience and expertise and creating the ability for excellence. You need to generate significant profit beyond the physical cost of your ECP.

In order to ensure a profitable return, it is important to carefully calculate all your business costs so you have a clear idea of your profit margin. This covers everything from travel, printing, training, phone calls, postage, advertising, marketing, networking, admin, accounting, tech/IT support, website design and hosting, branding, strategy etc. As well as equipment such as your computer, phone, printer, website, email hosting or brochures. Also, not forgetting the cost of running your "office", which may well be your home.

These costs are called overheads and there are two types of overhead expenses: direct and indirect.

Direct overheads

These overhead expenses are easy to calculate as they are the direct cost of your ECP. For example if you are a workman, building a kitchen for a customer, then the cost of the kitchen units themselves are a direct overhead. The cost is purely the result of the customer's order.

Indirect overheads

These are expenses that are not directly related to a customer's purchase, but without them your business couldn't function.

Website design fees, office heating costs and professional development costs are examples of indirect overheads. These overheads are trickier to calculate because they can be a monthly, annual or irregular expenses. These expenses need to be divided between each client's invoice to ensure the money is there when you need it.

Calculating your overheads is essential to calculating your profit margin. Once you know exactly how much it is costing you to do business, you can then set the price of your ECP.

Finding out how much comparable products and businesses are charging can be really helpful. This will often put you in the ballpark of the price you need to charge but don't trust this entirely. Just because another business is charging a certain amount, doesn't mean that they have accurately calculated their overheads or have the same business expenses as you. You need to be able to calculate these numbers independently. Head over to the Business of Blessing Study Guide now (available at www.businessofblessing.com) for a practical break-down on how to identify and calculate every possible overhead expense, and calculate your exact profit margin.

One of the most important but difficult expenses to calculate is your personal salary. How much per hour are you getting paid for each task that you undertake with your business? This is a complicated task. It is easy when an employer tells you how much he will pay you, it's a totally different ball game to decide how much you will get paid... and then ask a customer for that money!

There is the third overhead: "Income Overhead." This is the expense of your time and is NOT equivalent to an employed salary.

The minimum wage expectation for a self-employed person is significantly more than to their employed counterpart. As a self-employed business owner you do not receive sick pay or holiday pay, you are not paid over-time and you do not received paid training. You do not have a notice period so your income could disappear overnight at any time. You accept the full financial burden if things go wrong. You must play the role of manager, accountant, customer liaison, strategist, human resources, advertiser and legal advisor, covering all areas of planning, research, development, production, distribution, feedback, book keeping and product development. You basically need to fulfil every professional role there would usually be in a large company, all at once— and with no support, training, contract security or paid time off. This all adds up.

You absolutely cannot survive on the same level of minimum wage as your employed counterpart. As a minimum, a self-employed wage should be two-and-a-half times that of the national minimum, employed, hourly wage. This is the equivalent of a self-employed "living wage", that is, the minimally acceptable wage with which to sustain a very basic lifestyle.

Ideally you want to aim for a minimum of five times the national minimum employed hourly wage. This will give you a comfortable income, excess to begin saving for retirement, flexibility for unexpected admin jobs and paid planning time to move the business forward.

Sales Funnel

Did you know that a funnel is the single most essential item to have in any business arsenal? Your funnel will single-handedly determine how successful your business will grow. Don't worry, I haven't gone mad! A 'Sales Funnel' is just a modern term to describe your sales process. The image of a funnel is helpful because a funnel is larger at the top and becomes more refined and focused the further down you travel.

By creating a sales funnel, you consciously create a process to develop trust, education, attraction and filtration. The sales funnel is a journey of information which compels your ideal client to engage and spend, but repels your non-ideal client (those likely to be a drain on your resources or be unhappy with your product).

Over the years, I have identified 12 key stages of my own sales process:

The Sales Funnel Process

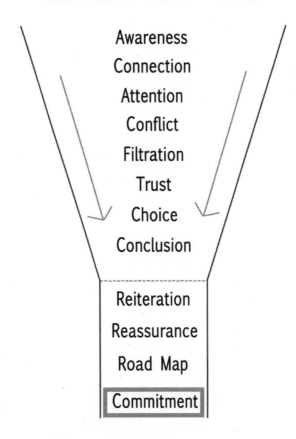

Awareness
Connection
Attention
Conflict
Filtration
Trust
Choice
Conclusion

Reiteration
Reassurance
Road Map
Commitment

Awareness

At the top of the sales funnel is 'Awareness'.

This is simply about letting as many people as possible know that your ECP exists. At this stage you are simply raising awareness of your business and what you offer.

After chatting with a friend of ours who runs a building company, he was so inspired by this concept that he began knocking on the doors of his client's neighbours when starting a new job. He introduced himself and explained that he would be doing some work a few doors down. He gave them his business card and told them to contact him if there were ever any problems or the van was in the way and he would move it immediately.

Genius!

It was never about the vans, but they gave him an excuse to make a non-salesy contact with a new prospective customer.

He sold his services, his professionalism, his trustworthiness, his diligence and he left his contact details, without them even realising he was actually advertising his business. They were even thankful for the contact.

So, when raising awareness of your business, along with traditional marketing methods, try to find as many creative ways as possible to reach your current customer's social circle. If they need your ECP later down the line, you want to make sure it is *your* name that springs to mind!

Connection

The next stage is connection with your potential client as a person. Who are they? What do they need? And, most importantly, what is their pain point?

Their pain point is a need, frustration or unfulfilled desire that they currently have in their life. This pain point connects their needs with their emotions. If you can trigger these emotions you can use this to make them look up from their busy life and be interested in what you can offer.

Attention

Now you have their attention you can explain what it is that you offer. How can your ECP meet their needs, fulfil their desires or enhance their life?

But be warned, the human attention span is not very long! People live busy lives and their greatest desire is for a quick fix, so don't waffle! Explain who you are and what you do in the simplest, quickest and most attractive way you can possibly think of— relating your description directly to what you know will interest them the most; their pain point!

Conflict

And now begins the conflict... no, not a physical conflict, put the boxing gloves down! The conflict is in your potential customer's head. Potential customers are not looking for reasons to buy, they are looking for a reason not to buy. They will begin to reason why they don't need your services, why they should be skeptical or how they could find a cheaper alternative. You need to address these concerns, ideally before they are even spoken. Anticipate their thought process and nip any negativity or doubt in the bud!

Filtration

Now your potential customer is onboard and fully understand what they are buying but this doesn't mean that they are automatically an ideal client for you. You need to engage in a process of 'Filtration'.

This is especially important if you are in a service-based industry and your time is limited. You can't afford to have a client who will dominate your time with unreasonable demands or be unsatisfied with your efforts.

Ask leading questions or make "Marmite" statements. For our friends outside the UK, Marmite is a uniquely tasting sandwich spread; some people love it and some people hate it. Marmite even utilised this polarised opinion and created an entire advertising campaign with the slogan, "*Marmite. You either love or hate it.*"

So, the Marmite effect is a description or question crafted to create a strong, polarised response in your prospective customer; they either love it or hate it!

Be clear, have a strong description about what you offer, how you work, who you work with and what to expect. These statements are not designed to attract everyone. To your ideal client it will be music to their ears, to your non-ideal client it will sound more like warning bells.

This is referred to as Branding. Branding is the subtle, but deliberate markers in your website, advertising and communication, that makes your ECP irresistible to your ideal customer but, at the same time, repel your non-ideal client.

Trust

By this stage your prospective customer probably wants to hear the price but we are not quite ready yet... we need to establish 'Trust'.

Trust is essential if a customer is ever going to purchase. They need to know that you are professional and that you are committed to excellence. They need to know that the product, their experience and the results are guaranteed. They need to trust, beyond a shadow of a doubt, that they will receive value for money before they hear the price.

This can be achieved through testimonies, qualifications or awards and communicating passion and commitment. It could be sample products or "loss leaders" (products that make a loss but entice customers to spend more in other areas of the business). It could be an introductory video or virtual tour. It could be a guarantee or membership to a regulatory body. It could be a smaller, cheaper product or service designed to build confidence for a larger purchase in the future.

Choice

Now you can present the 'Choice' of your main ECP.

What can they buy? What are the different pricing options? Is your product or service customisable? Remember, don't be tempted to offer more than three options. Too much choice will cause a delay in the decision-making process that could cost you the sale. Two or three options is perfectly adequate to meet a variety of potential needs.

Conclusion

During these first stages of the Sales Funnel you have been leading your prospective customer through a process of connection, trust, education and filtration towards a Conclusion. By this stage, they will know whether your ECP is right for them or not. You will not be the right choice for everyone. In fact, from all the people who ever come in contact with your business, it is usual to convert around 1-5% into paying customers. For some people, they simply don't need your service or product, for some, it is not exactly what they wanted, some can't justify the cost and for some it is just the wrong time. Do not worry about these people, let them go and focus instead on those who *are* ready to become paying customers.

At this point of conclusion the serious discussion begins. Time to go through the nitty, gritty logistics with the three R's: **Reiteration, Reassurance** and **Road Map**.

Reiteration

First of all, 'Reiterate' what you offer and exactly what your customer can expect from you and your ECP. This is an important stage that many new business owners skip, to their peril! It is important to make sure that the previous information has made sense and that your potential customer is definitely an ideal client and that they fully understand what they are buying. This process of reiteration is a crucial component for managing future expectation and eliminating the potential for conflict.

Reassure

'Reassure' your potential customer that you understand their needs and that you take your commitment to them very seriously. Potential customers will run a mile at the last hurdle if they feel that your only focus is their money, so reassure your commitment to treat them with care and provide value for money.

Road Map

Explain exactly what happens next; how do they purchase? How will they pay? How will you deliver? You are verbally taking your potential customer by the hand and leading them through the booking process so that they feel safe, informed and ready to commit.

Commitment

Which brings us to the final stage: Commitment... contracts are signed, money is exchanged and you can now get on with delivering an outstanding ECP to your new customer! Whoop, Whoop! This is the moment you have been waiting for and you can start doing the thing that you love.

Automating the Sales Funnel

Creating and delivering your ECP is the reason you went into business in the first place but, in reality, running a successful business (especially in the early days) means spending around 80% of your time creating a successful sales and marketing process and only 20% actually creating and delivering your product. The solution to release yourself more, is to automate this sales funnel as much as possible.

For my own business, I instinctively created a marketing strategy and a website that took the visitor through this process automatically. My website was designed to lead my visitors through the information needed for each of the sales funnel stages. This meant that by the time a prospective customer got in touch they were already at the 3 R's stage and we could quickly move to the commitment stage in just one email. This automated sales funnel meant that I could actually spend the vast majority of my time creating and delivering my ECP which was the thing that made me jump out of bed and love my job!

The key to creating a successful automated sales funnel is to step into your prospective customer's shoes and imagine that you have never heard of your business before and know nothing about your commitment to excellence. What would you need to hear in order to know that this is a reputable company, a superior product and represents value-for-money and customer-focused service?

As you address each stage of the sales funnel process on your website or marketing material, you will lead your customer towards their conclusion automatically.

Chapter 9

<u>The Dirty 'M' Word</u>

Can a Christian be Wealthy?

Your business has the potential to impact the world, not just in the direct value that you create through your ECP but, more importantly, through the profit you generate. When this profit is channeled into worthy causes, it has the potential to have a generational impact far beyond your business itself.

By shying away from generating profit you are actually limiting the potential for your business to contribute to change on a global scale. You can't give out of what you don't have. If you can generate significant profit, you can give on a significant level, it is as simple as that.

With one simple sentence, my husband Matt massively shaped my understanding, and comfort level, with the idea of profit. When we were still dating he said to me, *"There is a lot of money out there and I want as much as I can so I can give it to the people who need it."* I laughed because he sounded like a modern-day Robin Hood; robbing the rich to feed the poor. Matt has always had a very selfless attitude towards money.

From the start of our marriage he made it clear that I never had to ask him if I wanted to give money to anyone. *"That's what money is there for, to give away"* he said.

If I ever felt stirred to give money away I had his full support without even discussing the figures with him. He has inspired and challenged me so much over the years and it is this desire to generate significant income that has largely fuelled all our entrepreneurial endeavours.

Which desire do you think is most valued by God? The desire to only earn enough for ourselves or the desire to earn far beyond our own needs so that we can give generously and significantly to others? We consider it godly and honourable to work to feed our own families (which it is) yet often consider it sinful to earn far beyond our own needs. Even though, through excess finance, we can serve the needs of those around us and the financial needs of the kingdom even more.

As Christians we can struggle with the idea of earning in excess because it seems greedy. We can be paranoid about inadvertently committing the sin of loving money as described in 1 Timothy:

> "For the love of money is a root of all kinds of evil."
> **1 Timothy 6:10**

This is one of the single biggest reasons that Christians often struggle to create successful businesses. Christianity is about servanthood, generosity and self-sacrifice, so the prospect of generating profit can seem in direct conflict. But it is important to note that there is a huge difference between successful profit generation and worldly ambition. The bible never ever says that money itself is wrong, only the love of money. Money is not evil, money is amazing! Money can do so much good. Money can keep us well-fed, healthy and mobile. Money can keep us safe and warm and protected. Money can buy education which can increase wisdom and problem-solving abilities. Money can create rest and relaxation which can lead to creativity and patience. Money can connect us with others. Money can meet a variety of needs not just in our lives but in the lives of those around us. Money is exciting, money opens doors of opportunity and builds ideas into reality. Money can create freedom and, therefore, increase our ability to give in other ways. Money is not evil, money is a God-given resource. Money is a tool to create freedom, health, choice and rest in our lives and in the lives of others.

No, it is the love of money that is root of all evil. This is a different thing. The love of money is not about using money as a resource to create, sustain and connect but in allowing a practical desire to become an insatiable obsession.

> ### "Whoever loves money never has enough..."
> **Ecclesiastes 5:10**

The love of money is the constant feeling of lack; the fear of being without money, or the frustration at not having enough. It is when we refocus our trust and security from God— the giver of the money— onto the money itself.

> ### "Those who trust in their riches will fall..."
> **Proverbs 11:28**

The issue is not how much money you have but in your attitude of heart towards it. Is it an obsession? Do you never have enough? Do you spend so long getting more that you never have time to enjoy the money you do have? Are you fearful or forget to be generous because your mind is too full of your own desires? Do you feel peaceful when you have money but panicked when you don't? Do you only feel safe when you have money? Has money become your source of security rather than God?

The simple fact is that money never was, and never will be, your provider; God is.
Money is not your security; God is.
Money is not your sustainer; God is.
Money will not take care of you in your old age; God will.
Money does not bring peace; God does.
God gives us the ability to earn money to meet our daily needs, save for retirement and explore the world around us but the money itself is not the ultimate source of our provision. God is.
He provides through the resource of money and the ability to work but he also provides through his resource of the church, through others, through family and through true friendships. He also set the laws of nature in place so He is well within His rights and ability to break those laws when it suits Him too, providing in unexpected and miraculous ways! Money is not a measure of God's ability to provide for you. Whether you have a lot of money or just a little, it makes absolutely no difference to your security in God or his ability to provide for every single need that you have.

"Command those who are rich in this present world
not to be arrogant nor to put their hope in wealth, which is so uncertain,
but to put their hope in God,
who richly provides us with everything for our enjoyment."
1 Timothy 6:17

This verse doesn't say that possessing money is bad, in fact it explicitly says that money is there to be enjoyed. No, it specifically says that the problem is boasting or trusting in money. This is a heart condition. Paul (the writer of 1 Timothy) doesn't tell rich people to give up their riches but to not boast or trust in them. It is possible to have money and to be free from the love of money (which is the obsession for more or the fear of loss).

The obsession for more, or the fear of loss, is an affliction that is universal. Loving or trusting in money is not a condition exclusive to rich people. You can be rich and trust God completely and you can be poor and obsessed with money, forgetting to look to God for your provision.

I know for myself, I think a lot more about money when I don't have any, than I do when I have. When we have no money, our mind can be consumed by it; budgeting, calculating and worrying. When we have surplus money, we are free to think of the good we can do instead. Our thought-life changes from what we *need*, to what we can *give*. Which seems most Godly to you?

We can often mistakenly think that poverty is a godly attribute because of Jesus' words:

"Blessed are you who are poor, for yours is the kingdom of God."
Luke 6:20

But we see clearly in the book of Matthew, where this statement from Jesus is also quoted, that it actually reads:

"Blessed are the poor in spirit for theirs is the kingdom of Heaven."
Matthew 5:3

It is not about being physically poor but being poor in spirit; that is, not holding riches in your heart. The "poor in spirit" are those who know, in their heart, that they do not own anything. They acknowledge that they only have what God has loaned them, as a resource, to be used for maximum long-term good. In their heart, they don't lay claim to any physical possession.

When we acknowledge that God is our provider and that every good gift comes from Him (James 1:17), we are free to enjoy the resource of money without holding the love of it in our hearts. We are not fearful to lose it because we know that God is our provider, He gave us the money in the first place and He can give it again. Even if it doesn't happen in our expected timescale, we are completely at peace in the knowledge that God knows our needs and is committed to provide for us (Philippians 4:19).

When we are poor in spirit, not holding on to money as our provider, our identity, our fulfilment or our right, but acknowledging that every penny is a gift of God we are freed and compelled to be generous.

"Freely you have received; freely give."
Matthew 10:8

This is the heart of a person who does not love money. It is not about a lack of money, but holding the money you do have with an open hand, knowing that God has given it for a reason. When your heart's desire is to be a good steward of your money, then God can trust you with more. Your business will grow because success is not the answer to your prayer for your own gain alone, but as the answer to the your prayer to be generous, to be effective for the Kingdom and to be a channel for God's provision in the world.

"You do not have because you do not ask God.
When you ask, you do not receive,
because you ask with wrong motives, that you may spend what you get
on your pleasures."
James 4:2-3

When our sole focus is on acquiring gain for our own pleasures, this is a not a desire that God can bless. This is not to say that you can't be successful, the world is full of extremely successful business people who prove that financial success is not directly linked to a generous, servant heart. But, when your heart and motives are right before God, you create an invitation for God's blessing on your business in more creative ways than you can imagine. God can open doors of opportunity more easily than if you had tried opening them simply through your own effort. You can experience peace and rest and fulfilment in a way that would seem impossible if you felt the success of your business rested purely on your own shoulders.

"...the rich will fade away even while they go about their business."
James 1:11

For the business person focused on their own gain, every day in business is a strain. They struggle to make time for rest, for community and for relationship for fear that they will get left behind or will not reach their goals. It doesn't matter how close they get to their targets, or even if they exceed them, they are always worried about losing what they have, or can only see the next target and want that instead. They are never satisfied, they are never at peace. They lose themselves in the struggle. They fade away. They lose their identity, their relationships, their hobbies and their purpose.

"Such is the fate of all who are greedy for money; it robs them of life."
Proverbs 1:19 (NLT)

Their work becomes their identity. Their achievements and possessions become their purpose. Yet they never have the time to fully enjoy what they've gained. Even when they stop, they can't relax. They can't wind down from the tension of the fight... so they just keep fighting. They become incapable of implementing, appreciating or enjoying a healthy work/life balance. They can't switch their brain off. They become their job. Their life becomes their financial targets. They may get their money but there is no blessing in this lifestyle.

This is why stress-related health conditions are so prevalent in workaholics. Our bodies are not designed to sustain extended periods of stress and they will start to fail when forced to endure excessive stress levels. But being a workaholic doesn't only relate to the rich, it simply relates to anyone who places riches above their trust in God and their true purpose in life. Those who don't slow down enough to appreciate and fully enjoy the season they are in right now. Those who are constantly living with unfulfilled goals, focusing on what they don't have rather than what they do have.

When Matt and I were newly married, I was feeling the emotional strain of being self-employed. I couldn't stop my mind from focusing on every customer that I lost, every plan that didn't work and the million questions and insecurities over whether we really had what it took. Under Matt's encouragement I went to my happy place (the spa up the road) to rest, swim, relax and, most importantly, pray. I spent two blissful hours (that I could not afford to take) reading my bible, writing and declaring truth in my prayer journal, exercising and physically resting and I cannot describe the transformation!

I felt SO relaxed but, more importantly, I felt so full of faith. I had refocused my thoughts onto the actual source of our success— our loving Father. I believed that He is who He says He is and that He can do what He says He can. Not only could but would fulfil His promises to us. We were not alone, our ultimate success did not rest on our shoulders. Yes, we have to work diligently but there was a peace and rest that came with giving the results over to God.

"So neither the one who plants nor the one who waters is anything, but only God, who makes things grow."
1 Corinthians 3:7

We need to be diligent with the things we can do, and in faith for the things that only God can do. Learning to live in contentment is the key to doing this. Frustration and impatience will drive you to desperation and into the love of money, regardless of how much money you have.

No, the love of money is not dependent on how much money you have, the love of money is being more focused on building your house than building God's. It is highlighted when your desire for more money, or the fear of losing it, overpowers God's command to rest and maintain balance in your work, relationships and health. Do you feel more or less joyful, hopeful and fulfilled depending on how much money is in your bank account?

"Keep your lives free from the love of money
and be content with what you have,
because God has said,

"Never will I leave you;
never will I forsake you."
So we say with confidence,
"The Lord is my helper; I will not be afraid.
What can mere mortals do to me?"
Hebrews 13:5-6

Every time the love of money is specifically referred to in the Bible, it is directly linked to our trust in God for our future and contentment which leads to rest. This is a temptation for every single one of us.

"Watch out! Be on your guard against all kinds of greed;
life does not consist in the abundance of possessions."
Luke 12:15

Jesus says, "all kinds of greed." This is because greed is a sin with many forms and can afflict the rich and poor alike. Our challenge whether rich or poor is to place our future in the hands of God, not in our bank balance. This is a lifelong journey that is applicable no matter how much you have.
So let's go back to that verse in Timothy and look at what Paul is actually saying:

"Command those who are rich in this present world
not to be arrogant nor to put their hope in wealth, which is so uncertain,
but to put their hope in God,
who richly provides us with everything for our enjoyment."
1 Timothy 6v 17

Paul doesn't say it is wrong to have wealth but that we must acknowledge the source of our wealth, being grateful to the one who gave the money and the ability to earn the money in the first place. When we acknowledge that all our wealth is from God then we will live an open-handed life.

Paul finishes by saying, God "richly supplies us with all things to enjoy." God gives us money to enjoy. Money is not evil it is the love of money; the constant feeling of lack, the unhealthy obsession with more and placing your trust in money, that is sinful.

Money itself is great. Money is there to be enjoyed. God richly gives all things to be enjoyed, "all things" includes money. Money is a resource to be used for good but also to be enjoyed!

We are not called to avoid wealth, but only to remember who the ultimate source of our wealth is and to place our trust and boast in him alone.

"But remember the Lord your God,
for it is he who gives you the ability to produce wealth."
Deuteronomy 8:18

God is the one who gives you the ability to produce wealth, so using our God-given ability, with a thankful heart, is actually a form of worship. It is something we can pray for, practice and enjoy because it is God who has given it to us.

Chapter 10

The Rule of Four

The Biblical Framework for Attracting Finance

Hmmm... "Attracting finance" you say?

Don't worry! This isn't another 'claim it' prosperity gospel— *Believe for wealth and it will fall in your lap!* ...that's not for me. You will be relieved to know that "attracting finance" in the biblical sense is not about spiritually 'claiming' more, but is more about what you do with the money you already have. God isn't interested in giving you more so you can have more, He is interested in financing an army of believers to live for a cause greater than themselves. He is not looking for those who pray the best prayers but those who demonstrate the best stewardship of the resources they already have. When we show ourselves trustworthy with the resources we have, we demonstrate that God can trust us with more. It's how we steward the money we already have that opens the door to future financial provision.

We have four simple commands when it comes to our finances. If our heart is right and we obey these commands, it doesn't matter how much money we have, we have the blessing of God on our finances.

1) Finance the Church
2) Be Generous
3) Save for the Future
4) Enjoy Yourselves!

1
Finance the Church - Tithing

The first command is to tithe. This means giving a tenth of your income back to God in the form of a deliberate, costly gift into the house of God, His church. This is a hotly debated topic but I honestly don't know why!
Firstly, it is simply impossible to out-give God. No matter what we give to God, He always gives back abundantly more, so why would we not give?
Secondly, it is a clear biblical commandment:

> "Bring the whole tithe into the storehouse,
> that there may be food in my house."
> **Malachi 3:10**

The 'tithe' is a tenth as explained in Deuteronomy:

> "Be sure to set aside a tenth
> of all that your fields produce each year.
> Eat the tithe of your grain,
> new wine and olive oil, and the firstborn of your herds and flocks
> in the presence of the Lord your God
> at the place he will choose as a dwelling for his Name,

so that you may learn to revere the Lord your God always."
Deuteronomy 14:22-23

And in Leviticus:

"One tenth of the produce of the land...
belongs to the LORD and must be set apart to him as holy.
Leviticus 27:30 (NLT)

And Numbers:

"When you receive from the Israelites the tithe I give you as your
inheritance, you must present a tenth of that tithe as the Lord's
offering."
Numbers 18:26

I think you are getting the idea; tithing a tenth of our income, into the house of God, is very much in the Bible. The tithe is to support the running of the "tent of meeting" (the Church) and to support the priests (our pastors) so they are able to fulfil their job single-mindedly. It is also to ensure that there is "food in the house" so that the church can be generous too and meet the needs of the members, surrounding community and the world.

On a personal level, my tithe is a physical reminder to not trust in my gain but to continually look to God. We are literally putting our money where our mouth is and physically acknowledging that God is the giver of all that we have and that we trust Him for our future. We show our willingness of heart to not hold onto the money that He gives us but to continually live open-handed, looking to God for our provision. We are acknowledging that we do not rely on physical things more than we trust and rely on God (Luke 4:4, Deuteronomy 8:3)

Many Christians argue that this is an Old Testament requirement, part of the old law and isn't relevant to us today as we live in a new covenant with Christ. But, it is very clear to me that the principle of honouring God with our "first-fruits" is very much a New Testament principle too. Paul himself discussed this very argument... because we are now living under grace not the law, should we disregard the old law? He answered explicitly:

> "Do we, then, nullify the law by this faith?
> Not at all!
> Rather, we uphold the Law."
> **Romans 3:31**

And Jesus himself spoke about tithing in Matthew:

> "Woe to you, teachers of the law and Pharisees, you hypocrites!
> You give a tenth of your spices—mint, dill and cumin.
> But you have neglected the more important matters of the law—justice, mercy and faithfulness.
> You should have practiced the latter,
> without neglecting the former."
> **Matthew 23:23**

This, to me, could not be clearer. We are to understand that God is not looking for religious practice at the expense of love and generosity towards others, but, equally, our call to live lives of genuine love and generosity doesn't mean that we neglect to honour the 'blueprint' that God has already given us on how to live the best life. We are no longer under the law, in that we are no longer liable for our inability to live it flawlessly, because of Jesus, but this doesn't mean the principles and guidance within in the law are irrelevant. It is still wisdom, it is God outlining how life, the life He created, works best. How to be happiest, how society can flourish and how everyone can feel safe and valued.

We don't tithe because we have to, God does not need our money (Psalm 50:10-12). We tithe a tenth of our income for three reasons:

Focus

We are declaring to our own hearts that God is the source of everything we own. He has only loaned it to us to meet our physical needs in this life. We hold no right to it and if God asks for it back, through either a tithe, generosity to a neighbour or through an unexpected loss, we are happy. We trust that God will continue to be our provider. He gave us this much, He can give it again. He has been faithful this time, He will continue to be faithful. Tithing focuses our heart and mind on God's generosity, faithfulness and power rather than being consumed with the facts and figures of our needs and desires.

Provision

There are practical needs within the church. The building needs maintenance, the heating bill doesn't pay itself. The equipment, the resources, the staff, the carpet, the chairs, the coffee, the cables, the emails, the website, the phone line... I could literally fill this whole chapter with a single list of the expenses that a church faces. This money doesn't grow on trees and God will not magic this money out of thin air. Why? Because he has already commanded His people to take care of it. He has already instructed us to be diligent and deliberate in our tithing to the church so that there is plenty to cover all of these needs. Not only this, but with ample provision within the church, the church as a whole is more able to meet the needs of the members, the surrounding community and the world. We tithe so the church can be generous too.

Promise
There is a promise attached the tithing. The only place, in the entire bible, that God challenges us to test Him! We invite God's supernatural provision when we let go of our tight grip on our finances.

> "Bring the whole tithe into the storehouse,
> that there may be food in my house.
> Test me in this,"
> says the LORD Almighty,
> "and see if I will not throw open the floodgates of heaven
> and pour out so much blessing
> that there will not be room enough to store it."
> **Malachi 3:10**

Wow, that is a big promise and a clear challenge! There are many Christians who spend a lot of time debating and trying to disprove the necessity of tithing but I tell you, they are missing out! I have seen God's faithfulness first-hand when we place obedience and giving at the forefront of our finances. The reality of biblical finances works. You can never out-give God. Whatever you give He will give you back more than you can ever imagine!

When my parents were young and newly married when they discovered this command to tithe. *"How can we do it?"* they thought. "*We are going into debt every month, we don't have enough as it is.*"

Never-the-less, they decided to obey. After all, God was laying down the challenge to test Him! They began to tithe, 10%, every month... and the most remarkable thing started to happen.

Nothing changed in their income and yet suddenly, every month, they had enough money. They were no longer going into debt, not by getting more money, but by giving more away. This is God's economy. It doesn't make sense, it doesn't work on paper, but it works in reality. I know this for a fact.

As you know, when Matt and I were first married, we had nothing. Money was so tight I couldn't afford the bus fare into the city to meet my friend for lunch. We considered asking my family to cover our petrol money to get home for Christmas, instead of presents, because I honestly didn't know how we were going to be able to afford it. In those days, tithing was not a virtual exercise of simply transferring money between bank accounts. I was being paid in cash and I tithed in cash. Having the money in my hand (money that we desperately needed), made the act of tithing even more poignant. I had to physically hand over to God a portion of the cash that I desperately needed. We didn't have enough and we could not afford to give this money to God but, in the spiritual realm, we couldn't afford to *not* give.

If we ever needed to be living under the blessing of God with our finances, it was then! If we ever needed to position ourselves to receive God's supernatural provision, it was then! We tithed with joy, we knew God would be true to his promise... and he was. Every single month we had enough money... and every month it was a surprise!

We had opportunities and connections that were simply miraculous. We had generous friends who created work for us. We had unexpected tax rebates and gifts, and our business revenue grow monumentally faster than it should have.

Only three months after our wedding, we were invited to go to America from the UK (where we live) to meet some of Matt's family who I had never met. This was an outrageous notion given the dire state our finances. But we knew that whatever vessel of faith you bring to God He will fill it, if you bring a cup He will fill it, if you bring a bath, He will fill that instead!

So, we opened a separate bank account and prayed, *"Father, we would really love to go to America for this special family holiday. In the natural, there is no way we can afford this but we know that You are the God of the supernatural. The trip is eight months away so, if we can go, we need to be able to put X amount of money into this account, in addition to the regular amount that we need for our living costs please."*

Well, what do you suppose happened?

Do you think we get the full amount in eight months?

No.

We got it in three months!!!

In just three months we had covered all our bills and been able to save the full amount that we needed for this family holiday. God completely exceeded our expectation and even our request, as if he was laughing saying, *"Eight months you say? You think I need eight months? ...Watch this!"*

We were living in God's economy now, and it worked. The more you give the more you receive.

Now, I am not saying that God will necessarily give you physical money when you give, like a slot machine – put money in, turn the dial and out pours the windfall – that's not how it works. That thinking completely misses the heart behind tithing. We mustn't make demands on God as if he is a magic genie. Remember, the whole point of giving back to God is to protect ourselves from the temptation to get caught in the love of money and how much more we want to have.

It is not about calculating how much God owes us back, it is about trusting God to provide for our every need and He will. But God is far too creative to be bound to simple coins alone, He finds a million creative, amazing and unexpected ways to provide. Doors of opportunity may open quicker than they would have. Elderly appliances seem to soldier on unendingly, refusing to break. Relationships and connections are introduced at just the right moment. Unexpected gifts can appear out of nowhere. God has a myriad of creative ways that He will use to provide for you. The one thing we can be certain of is that He WILL provide. But the additional ease and provision may be forfeited if we refuse to place our financial trust in God completely.

"You expected much, but see, it turned out to be little.
What you brought home, I blew away.
Why?" declares the Lord Almighty. "Because of my house, which remains a ruin,
while each of you is busy with your own house.
Therefore, because of you
the heavens have withheld their dew and the earth its crops.
I called for a drought on the fields and the mountains,
on the grain, the new wine, the olive oil and everything else the ground produces, on people and livestock,
and on all the labor of your hands."
Haggai 1:9-11

Wow. This verse blows me away every time. We always need to be challenged and reminded to make the focus of our lives, our success and our finance, on the building of God's house instead of our own. Yes, we need to build our own house— this is wisdom and diligence— but the challenge is whether we are more concerned about building our own house rather than God's?

I had a friend who recently confided in me how difficult her finances were. She said, "My husband and I both have good jobs and are on good incomes but we just can't seem to save. We have so many dreams but we can never afford to get there. There is always something that comes up— an expected big expense or bill. It is relentless, and means we are never able to achieve our goals."

My first thought was to ask her, "Do you tithe?"

"No," she said, "we can't afford to tithe because we are not reaching our financial goals as it is."

But the question is not whether we can afford to tithe, but whether we can afford _not_ to tithe?

When we place our own house above God's house we miss out on a blessing in our finances. There is a robbing of the ease and blessing that exists when living in obedience. Appliances break, emergencies and unexpected bills mount up and your money just slides through your fingers like sand. Things are hard, there is a stagnation, our lives consumed with fear and frustration. No amount of money is ever enough. But when we place God, and His house, as the top priority in our finances, we invite a blessing. We invite his provision and we invite the miraculous. This may not happen overnight— although I have had many times when it has— but we have an assurance that as we continue to be obedient in the small things, He will provide and sustain us in the big things.

145

And this is where the blessing goes further, to something far more precious: peace.

The people responded to this challenge brought by the Prophet Haggai in the verse we just read, by changing their ways and refocusing on building the temple. God then began to speak courage and promise to them.

"Be strong... and work.
For I am with you... do not be afraid."
Haggai 2:4-5

"'In this place I will grant peace,'
declares the Lord Almighty."
Haggai 2:9

This is far more precious than gold or silver; we receive a place of peace, not only within the temple but also in this new way of life. When we let go of our finance, let go of our striving, worrying and wanting, we open our hearts to receive God's courage and promise. We will live in peace. This is the promise and I am one of many, many faithful believers all over the world who know this to be true. Test Him in this and see if He will not open the flood gates of heaven and pour out so much blessing that you will not have room for it all!

2

Be Generous

This is the next command with our finances: remember the poor. Live generous lives. Look after each other. Meet the needs of others in the most generous way that you possibly can.

*"Generosity brings prosperity,
but withholding from charity brings poverty.
Those who live to bless others
will have blessings heaped upon them,
and the one who pours out his life to pour out blessings
will be saturated with favour."*
Proverbs 11:24-25 (TPT)

This is in addition to our tithe to build the house of God. The command to be generous is not the same as making sure there is resource within the house of God. These are separate commands. We tithe the "first fruits" to church as an act of faith and obedience. We give to those around us because we are able. We live generous lives because we ourselves have been blessed. No matter how tight things are there is always someone who is struggling more. The command to live generous lives is there to open our eyes to those around us, to soften our hearts to the needs of others. It is there so that we begin to see those around us as God sees them. We see their value and we feel the heart of God to provide for them. We are the hands and feet of Jesus in this world. What good is it to simply pray for God to provide when He can give us the resource to meet that need ourselves? It is easy for God to give money to you, but the real question is, how easily can God give money through you?

*"Therefore, I command you to be open handed toward your fellow
Israelites who are poor and needy in your land."*
Deuteronomy 15:11

Live life with an open hand, ready to give to anyone in need. Plan to be generous, prepare for it. Whether it is a neighbour or friend or a stranger, live life with eyes open to see how you can meet the needs of those around you, through the blessing that God has given you.

Through observing and praying into my own giving over the years, I have identified three levels of generosity in my own life:

Basic Generosity

This is day-to-day generosity, 'loose change' generosity (being spontaneously generous with the loose coins in your pocket). It is buying a drink, opening my home, cooking a meal, giving a gift, helping a stranger. This is basic generosity that I am able to do every day at very little cost to myself, other than the thoughtfulness it took to do something nice for someone. It is generosity in the small things.

Intentional Generosity

This is above and beyond basic generosity. It is the level of generosity that requires planning, saving, setting money aside, setting up direct debits, budgeting and sometimes going without in order to create finance to meet someone else's need.

* Choose charities and commit to fund them.
* Sponsor children through development programmes.
* Plan and save for larger annual gifts to your local church, over and above your tithe, to enable the church to buy buildings, employ more staff and to move forward in reaching the needs of the community.
* Set money aside each month to meet any unexpected needs for those around you.

Right from the start of our businesses Matt and I set aside "generous money" every month, in addition to the regular money we have committed to charitable giving. Even when we were tight on money ourselves we set aside a small amount every month with the focused intention of keeping our eyes and ears open for any need in our community. If we didn't hear of anything, we asked God to tell us who to give the money to and gave it as a surprise. Over the years it has been such a fun exercise. It forces us to keep our eyes open to those around us and to be quick to respond to any need that we see. We became addictively excited for our potential to become an answer to prayer for someone else and this still drive our businesses today.

Outrageous Generosity

This is wild generosity. Generosity that in the natural we cannot afford; giving away major assets, giving beyond our budget, giving up our savings for a car, a house or future retirement. This is the kind of generosity that leaves you in a position of significant need yourself. This is not generosity to rush into. As we have read, the Bible is extremely clear that we must be wise, methodical and forward-planning in our finances. Outrageous generosity will come with a clear prompt from God. You will feel no doubt that God is calling you to do this and feel at peace and even excited!

I have had only a few times that God has asked me to do this in my life and I have been obedient. Every single time, He has faithfully provided above and beyond what I sacrificed. If God calls you to do this in some way, he will always, always provide for you above and beyond what you expected. This may not be a weekly or even a yearly prompt but live a life that is open to the call to outrageous generosity. Do not fear it; it is the most amazing opportunity to see the undeniably miraculous provision of God.

Whether in basic day-to-day generosity, the strategy of intentional generosity or occasional outrageous generosity, the main attitude of heart is to be eager and joyful to give whenever you can, to whoever you can. Give knowing that you can never out-give God. When you give, you not only honour and please Him but you position yourself for blessing. God can't help himself, His heart is bursting with generosity. He loves to give and He loves to reward cheerful and trusting generosity.

"Give and it will be given to you.
Good measure, pressed down, shaken together, running over,
will be poured into your lap.
For with the measure you use, it will be measured back to you."
Luke 6:38

God cannot bless a tight-fisted believer. God's economy does not work like the world economy. In the world's economy, you profit by gaining, in God's economy, you profit by giving; pressed down, shaken together, running over and pouring into your lap! Focus on giving and God will provide the resource because he knows that no matter how much he gives you, you will continue to channel it into the need he wants to meet.

3

Plan for the Future

The third command is to be diligent with our finance. To be wise and forward-thinking; preparing for the future, providing for your family and for your children's children. Plan financially for the expenses of the future, and keep an intensional watch on the state of your finances. In Proverbs we are told that we are wise if we consider the ways of the ant. Ants are focused and hardworking in their preparation. They get all they can in each season and store it away to provide for the colony.

"Take a lesson from the ants...
Learn from their ways and become wise!
... they labor hard all summer,
gathering food for the winter."
Proverbs 6:6,8 (NLT)

We are told to be diligent and strategic in our accounting:

"Invest in seven ventures, yes, in eight;
you do not know what disaster may come upon the land."
Ecclesiastes 11:2

We have already looked at this verse from the context of being wise and balanced with investments but there is also an assumption here. There is an expectation that we will be investing for the future, planning to be able to financially 'ride out' any calamity that may happen. We don't know what the future holds, how economics will shift, how society will change or if our health may deteriorate. We need to look to build up income to protect against such eventuality. There are many other verses urging us to be wise and focused in our preparation for the future:

"A good man leaves an inheritance to his children's children."
Proverbs 13:22

"But if anyone does not provide for his relatives,
and especially for members of his household,
he has denied the faith."
1 Timothy 5:8 (ESV)

"The wise have wealth and luxury, but fools spend whatever they get."
Proverbs 21:20 (NLT)

"...whoever gathers money little by little makes it grow."
Proverbs 13:11

"Wisdom protects us just as money protects us..."
Ecclesiastes 7:12 (GW)

Money is given to you as a resource to protect yourself.
Protect yourself from the elements with safe housing, clothes and heat etc.
Protect yourself from ill-health by eating a balanced diet and getting the medical care you need.
Protect yourself from boredom by engaging your passions.
Protect yourself from isolation by providing for your travel and social expenses.
Protect yourself from stagnation by facilitating your mission within the Church.
Protect yourself from exhaustion by buying rest and relaxation.
This doesn't just mean in your working life but planning to use money for this protection in your retirement too. Have a longterm view with your finances.

"A rich man's wealth becomes like a citadel of strength,
but the poverty of the poor leaves their security in shambles."
Proverbs 10:15 (TPT)

Part of planning for the future involves making sure that you are living within your means now. You can't save for the future if you don't have excess to save with. If you are spending everything you get every month, welcoming debt, stretching your budget as tight as it will go or living beyond your means for the sake of your own comfort then you are not fulfilling the command to prepare yourself and your family for the future.

"Whoever loves pleasure will become poor;
whoever loves wine and olive oil will never be rich."
Proverbs 21:17

Find ways to cut down, cut back or cut out.
Cut down the frequency of your spending, cut back on the cost of the products you choose or cut out the spend entirely if you could actually live without that expense.
Be honest with yourself. Create budgets with plenty of excess so that you have plenty to cover your needs now and the needs of the future. This may mean swapping the gym membership for jogging around your estate, moving to a cheaper house or to a cheaper area. It may mean cutting down on take-outs, swapping designer clothes for white label or doing your own beauty treatments. It may mean taking long walks or holidays in your own country or staying with friends. It may mean cooking from scratch, selling the second car or taking lunch to work. Save instead of spending wherever possible. No matter how small, make the changes you need to live a life with plenty of money left over.
If you are not being a good steward of your money now, consistently spending beyond your means or wasting your money frivolously, there is no way God can trust you to be a wise steward of additional finance. So, make sure you are

planning for the future as well as providing for your current needs.

> "Our people must learn to devote themselves to doing good
> so that they may provide for urgent needs
> and not live unproductive lives."
> **Titus 3:14**

4
Enjoy Yourself

The final command is a fun one... enjoy yourself! Loosen up, embrace life, indulge in some "me-time". You have paid your tithe to commit your money to God. You have opened your heart and your hand to be generous to those in need. You have provided for daily necessities and put money aside for the future, so with what is left, live a little!

Take that trip you've been dreaming of, treat yourself to some new clothes, go to the theatre, buy nice food, get a massage or a new gadget, indulge a new hobby, learn a new skill... the world is literally your oyster!

Have fun and dream big.

> "This is what I have observed to be good:
> that it is appropriate for a person to eat, to drink
> and to find satisfaction in their toilsome labor under the sun
> during the few days of life God has given them,
> for this is their lot.
> Moreover,
> when God gives someone wealth and possessions,
> and the ability to enjoy them,

154

to accept their lot and be happy in their toil—
this is a gift of God.
They seldom reflect on the days of their life,
because God keeps them occupied with gladness of heart."
Ecclesiastes 5:18-20

God wants us to be occupied with a gladness of heart. It may come as a surprise to read that gladness of heart is linked to eating, drinking, working and the ability to enjoy wealth!

Of course, at its heart, true joy comes from being thankful and trusting in God the Father, and it is entirely possible to experience a life of tangible delights and still be extremely unhappy if your heart's focus is out of alignment.

But when the focus of our heart is gratitude for God's past provision and peaceful faith for tomorrow's, we are released to rest, relax and enjoy today.

Ecclesiastes says that the ability to enjoy wealth is a gift of God.

Enjoy learning, enjoy resting and enjoy new experiences.

Enjoy new foods and new sensations.

Enjoy adrenaline and adventure.

Enjoy exploring and nesting.

Enjoy being immersed in new cultures and breathing in the wonder of God's creation.

Enjoy good food and a little pampering.

Enjoy hobbies and explore your curiosity.

Do the things that make you happy. God has created a big and beautiful world out there. Why? To be explored. So we can marvel at His wonder and have our God-breathed creativity inspired.

He has given us tastebuds for a reason. So we can take pleasure in eating. He has made us to enjoy the feeling of water on our skin, lying in the sun, snuggling in a duvet, adrenaline, challenge and gazing out over breathtaking mountains. He has made us to be curious, to love experience and adventure. He wants us to enjoy our lives, to soak up all the amazing aspects of this life He has created. He needs us to rest and recharge so we can more effective for Him. He needs us to be inspired so we can create the visions He places in us. He needs us to be comforted so that we have the reserves to give out to others. He needs us to be excited so we can spread the joy of life to others. He loves to see us enjoying his creation because as we do that, and live life to the full with a grateful heart, we are acknowledging His almighty wonder, His greatness, His power, his creativity, His faithfulness and His beauty.

Finding joy and fulfilment in our lives with a heart full of gratitude to God, is actually a form of worship. We praise and thank God by enjoying what he has created.
I have the most amazing and creative Dad and he was always building fantastic climbing frames and treehouse for us. As he built, the sole thought in his mind was how excited we would be, and the many hours of fun we would have as we climbed and played, learning and laughing, until we eventually collapsing into a blissful, satisfied sleep. How disappointed would he be if we didn't want to enjoy the wonderland he had created? There is no joy in watching us be miserable and sedentary. One of the greatest joys of parenthood is giving your children new experiences and activities they will love. If this is how earthly parents feel, how much more does God feel like this (Matthew 7:11).

Enjoy the experiences He has given us, explore opportunities and thrive on adventure. Grow, learn, laugh and explore. Enjoy yourself. It is okay to relish the feeling of a warm sea or the beauty of a barrier reef, to marvel at a tropical sunset or the majesty of snow-capped mountains. It is okay for adventure and relaxation to make your heart sing. God has designed it to have this effect. When we are enjoying ourselves, within the boundaries God has given us, then God is enjoying Himself too. He takes joy in our pleasure and delights in our excitement. Enjoying ourselves without gratefulness or acknowledgement of God leads to disappointment and emptiness but enjoying life with the thankful heart to the provider of such pleasure is a fullness of life that only a believer can know.

"Who can eat or enjoy themselves without God?"
Ecclesiastes 2:25 (GW)

It is God himself who gives the ability to truly enjoy life and all the pleasures, experience and fun on offer.

"He continued,
"Go home and prepare a feast, holiday
food and drink;
and share it with those who don't have anything:
This day is holy to God.
Don't feel bad.
The joy of God is your strength!"
Nehemiah 8:10 (MSG)

The context of this verse about finding joy in God is about finding pleasure in life. Finding joy in the world around us and in the simple pleasures that He has provided like eating,

157

drinking, feasting, holidays and celebrations. God has given us the little things in life to bring us joy, bring us pleasure, give us comfort and rest and bring us excitement. Just like an earthly father he wants us to enjoy these little gifts, seize life and live it to the full. God doesn't want us to live miserable, restricted and uninspired. Allow the simple pleasures of life to bring you joy and thankfulness and you will live the kind of happy and contented life that best reflects God to those who don't know Him.

"A joyful heart is good medicine..."
Proverbs 17:22

The Three-Point Principle

As with all things, the key is moderation. John Wesley perfectly summed this up when he said,

"Gain all you can, give all you can and save all you can."

The Rule of Three: gain, give, save.
"Gain all you can" refers to productivity and wise investment but ultimately it is about gaining things for yourself so it can be applied to gaining experience, adventure, learning and relaxation for yourself also. It is not wrong to achieve gain for yourself as long as it is not at the expense of your responsibilities. The balance is to not use your finances to gain so much experience and fun that you neglect your responsibility to save for the future, be generous and be faithful in your commitment to your local church.

158

Equally, don't give so much away that you leave yourself and your family in need or you live a boring, mediocre life.

In the same way, don't save so much that you forget to be generous and forget to have fun.

All three must be present and in balance, so that you can live free, fulfilled, obedient and wise, living life to the full with a clear conscience and a thankful heart.

Chapter 11

<u>A Good Tree Produces Good Fruit</u>

Seven Foundations of Biblical Business

I found myself feeling stressed.

I had so many dreams for my business, so many targets not yet reached, so much excitement and anticipation and longing. I am a forever dreamer. It's the way I am wired. I get excited about possibility and tenacious about action. This strong quality gets things done. It is a God-given attribute that has benefitted my own business and the businesses of many others. But, as with all good attributes, there is a flip side. A good side and a bad side. Situations that I am adept to handle and other situations that I don't cope well with at all. In this instance, the flip side was impatience. I am such a "doer" and action-taker, that I often find myself extremely impatient. Instead of living in the joy of my season I am tempted to live in my future imaginings and then feel frustrated that they are not yet reality. I am keenly aware of my failing in this area and the need to keep this "flip side" under control... and most of the time I do.

However, this was not one of those days.

I found myself glum, frustrated and hopeless. I was impatient and discouraged. I felt like giving up.

"I think my business is failing," I solemnly declared to Matt. To which, he immediately laughed, pulling me out of my stupor.

"You are too funny," he said, *"...failing?! You are get five times more enquiries and bookings than many others in our industry and have just this week booked another dream client. What on earth are you talking about?"*

I had to laugh at myself too. How unreliable our feelings can be! How disconnected from reality! And how important to realise that when we focus on what don't have, instead of what we do, our perception of reality can warp. We can feel discouraged when actually we have so much to be thankful and content about.

That very week I read a verse that has become my business mantra. Every time I find myself slipping into impatience, I speak this verse aloud to myself.

"A good tree produces good fruit..."
Matthew 7:17 (CEV)

I realised something life changing when I read this verse. Something that had the power to transform my business life, and yours too.

I realised that my only responsibility is to grow a good tree and it is God who brings the fruit. He has ordained that from a good tree comes good fruit. It is law of nature; predictable and reliable.

I don't need to worry and strive for the fruit; willing it to grow and desperately trying to shape and control it. No, I only need to relax and focus on building a healthy, strong foundation. Building a good root system, that will feed my business with the nutrients it needs to produce good fruit. The fruit will come all by itself as I focus on creating the right foundation and making sure that my business is healthy.

So what does it look like to have a healthy business? There are many key foundations that, when put into place in your business, will cause it to grow strong and healthy. Here are my top seven:

1
Servanthood

It is too easy when self-employed to become a workaholic without even realising it. Many people set out to build their own business because they want to be in control of their own timetable, but end up feeling like a slave to it, working all hours and pulling back from church service.

"He saw at the water's edge two boats,
left there by the fishermen, who were washing their nets.
He got into one of the boats, the one belonging to Simon, and asked him to put out a little from shore. Then he sat down and taught the people from the boat.
When he had finished speaking, he said to Simon,
"Put out into deep water, and let down the nets for a catch."
Simon answered,
"Master, we've worked hard all night and haven't caught anything.
But because you say so, I will let down the nets."
When they had done so, they caught such a large number of fish that their nets began to break.

> So they signalled their partners in the other boat to come and help them, and they came and filled both boats so full that they began to sink."
>
> **Luke 5:2-7**

I bet you have heard this story a million times and, just as many times, have asked yourself the same question we all do: 'What does it mean to put down my nets again? What does this look like in my life?"

We want the supernatural haul that Simon experienced but let's back up a minute. There was something very important that happened between Simon having a bad night's 'business' and Jesus providing miraculous, supernatural provision. Simon served.

Simon was on the shore washing his nets; this was his to-do list. We all have a long to-do list. It doesn't matter if your business is a day old or a decade old, the to-do list doesn't get any shorter. Simon's business was not going as well as he needed it to. He had not caught enough fish so his income had significantly dropped overnight. He was, no doubt, worried and stressed and keen to get back out fishing and see if he could reverse his fortunes.

But along comes Jesus. Very inconveniently, Jesus asks Simon to put aside his to-do list and serve him instead. He asks Simon to take him out in his boat so he could teach the crowds. Now we know that Jesus was not a quick preacher. This was likely to be at least two hours, probably more!

The whole time that Jesus was preaching, hour after hour, what was Simon doing? Just sitting there! He had plenty of time to look at his unprepared nets (his unfinished to-do list) calculating exactly how far behind he was falling and what this would mean for his business. But he stayed right there, putting

163

aside his worry and his to-do list and focusing on facilitating Jesus' message to the crowd.

The same is true for each one of us in business. We will always have a long to-do list. Don't kid yourself by saying, "It's just a season I'm in, I'll serve once my business is working better." It never will! If you build a foundation of prioritising your to-do list, no matter how much better things get in the future, you will never find the time to serve. There will always be things that seem more pressing, more satisfying or more rewarding than serving, but you will be missing out. You will be missing out on the supernatural, miraculous provision that can result from placing the mission of Jesus ahead of your own needs.

Keep connected to the mission of Jesus. Keep connected to your local church. Serve and share with the people of God. Whatever that looks like for you. You will need to find areas of service in the church that are practical but once you start looking you will find lots!

I am often travelling for work on the weekends so I serve on the welcome team because it is flexible to my availability. I also love this team and I'm good at it. I'm good at making sure each person feels valued and welcomed as they walk through the door so this is a good position for me to serve in.

I serve on the New Christians team, praying with those who make a decision for Jesus on a Sunday morning. It is no effort at all, I mean: is this not the greatest honour any Christian can have?

I serve mid-week, hosting (and for a time, overseeing) the home groups. I am on the pastoral team and invest time helping others. I open my home and my life. I have picked up litter before a service and restocked toilet paper. I take stock inventory of our resource cupboard and take out the trash. I've polished the banisters and painted the conference room. I've planned and taught Home Group Leaders' training sessions, taught on the Alpha courses and our church Engage course.

Once you start looking you will find many ways that you can serve within church and still maintain your business. It doesn't really matter what you do as long as you do something! By putting aside your to-do list, and focus on playing your part in facilitating the mission and message of Jesus through the local church, you open your life to the potential for supernatural provision in your business.

You may find, just like Simon, that by taking time out from your business to serve in church, God actually provides an increase that did not even rely on getting your to-do list finished in the first place! We will experience an ease and supernatural increase and progression that exceeds anything we could have achieved. I can't wait to hear the stories you will have when you put this in place.

2

Community

Similarly, make time for family and friends. Make time for relationships. Only last week Matt and I had hit a roadblock in our online-coaching business. We could NOT find software that operated in the way we needed it to. Matt had spent days researching and emailing various tech supports but to no avail!

We brought it to God and said, "Lord, we trust you. If this is the right thing to do then we really need you to come through for us and show us a way forward by the end of the day. If not, we will change the format of what we are planning, even though it doesn't seem as good, and trust that this is the right thing to do."

That very afternoon I was spending time with a friend. This friend has no understanding of our industry and had never run a business before. Yet, when I casually mentioned the dilemma we were facing, she said, "Why don't you do this idea...?"

Immediately I ran and asked Matt and he confirmed that this was indeed a viable way forward and potentially could be even better than what we had planned!

If that is not an encouragement to make time for community, I don't know what is. Matt and I were under a lot of stress trying to figure out a solution to our problem, we brought it to God and then took time out to build relationships and out of the blue, our answer to prayer came through a friend.

This is the value of connection. As we invest into relationships, God can invest into us. God loves to speak through people. He loves to answer prayer through people. By isolating yourself, you isolate yourself from an aspect of God's voice. Give of yourself to others, not looking to gain anything back but simply building others up... and you may find that, in more ways than one, God builds you up too!

"And let us consider how we may spur one another on toward love and good deeds, not giving up meeting together, as some are in the habit of doing, but encouraging one another."
Hebrews 10:24-25

3
Diligence

Be organised. God loves order, because order brings peace (1 Corinthians 14v33) God cannot bring the fullness of His blessing on disorder. Being organised and diligent is actually an expression of our love for God and our understanding of the role we play in facilitating his peace here on earth.

"Everything must be done properly and in an orderly way."
1 Corinthians 14:40 (GW)

You can't run a disorderly business— avoiding deadlines, missing client emails, miscalculating profit margins, rushing the forward planning or mis-managing resources— and expect the fullness of God's blessing on your business. Neither can God bless it when we put off harder, necessary tasks to focus only on easier, less productive tasks.

"Don't waste your time on useless work..."
Ephesians 5:15 (MSG)

Being "busy" in order to avoid other necessary tasks?
Ouch! I know, I do that too!
One of the hardest things about being self-employed is that we have to be good at everything. When employed you have the opportunity of focusing solely on the task that you are employed to do, the tasks that you show a natural aptitude for. When self-employed you don't have this luxury.
When self-employed, the buck stops with you. You must learn to do everything: accounts, business plans, websites, Facebook ads, design, packaging and developing a sales process. You must learn how to be a marketeer, advertiser, salesman, presenter, accountant and tech support all at the same time. You are intimately involved with every hurdle of product development, manufacturing and distribution, profit generation, advertising, professional networking and market analysis. It is exhausting and hard, I know! But with God there is a way forward. There are solutions and empowerment. There are divine connections, people to learn from and companies to outsource to. Plus, through prayer, you may even surprise yourself with how much more you can learn and do.

At the end of the day, you just have to stick at it. Force yourself to tackle every task in front of you, no matter how scary, and prayerfully look to God for His guidance and enabling. Make the best, most productive use of your time. Plan your day and slowly chip away at the more difficult, less desirable tasks, even just 20 minutes a day. By working little and often on the tasks you hate, you'll be surprised how much you can achieve by the end of the month.

God loves a hard worker. He loves diligent workers who plan ahead and take care of all the little things.

"Be sure you know the condition of your flocks, give careful attention to your herds."
Proverbs 27:23

"Do not be unwise but wise, making the best use of your time."
Ephesians 5:15-16 (ISV)

"Take full advantage of every day..."
Ephesians 5:16 (TPT)

"All hard works brings a profit, but mere talk leads only brings poverty."
Proverbs 14:23

4

Purpose

Have a bigger picture. Why do you want to build a business of your own in the first place? Having a bigger plan, an ultimate purpose, will help keep you going in the hard times and help keep you on track. A bigger purpose will help remind you of the most important things in life. You are here for a purpose: God's purpose in and through you.

"I cry out to God Most High, to God who fulfils his purpose for me."
Psalm 57:2 (ESV)

Your purpose on this earth is about so much more than running a business. You are so much more than your job title and your life must be about more than simply generating your desired income. What does God's purpose look like in your life? Your purpose is to be effective and active in the body of Christ, the Church, to help bring the Kingdom of God here on earth. Our purpose is to be a channel for His provision and become His answer to prayer for others. We are to build healthy relationships and healthy families, who laugh, have fun and love each other. We are to enjoy and worship through all our experiences. We are to live healthy lives, looking after the body we have been given. We are to love the poor and open our homes to everyone.

"Where there is no vision, the people perish."
Proverbs 29:18 (KJV)

Without clear purpose in your business, you will slip silently into stress, striving and frustration. You will become so consumed with the challenges and demands of the season that you will forget to look up and delight in the blessings of today. You forget to implement the foundations of your purpose into your life right now.

Live a life today that reflects the purpose you want for tomorrow. As an outsider looking in, would it be clear what your purpose really is? Would it be obvious, by how you choose to spend your time, money and energy, what the true purpose of your business is? Do not wait until later to live in that purpose because, I guarantee, that perfect day will never come. You will have created such a strong habit of working endlessly that you will lose the ability to rest and enjoy living in your purpose.

Do you hope to have more time with your family? Make that time now.

Did you want to give more to church? Start giving now.

Did you want to have more time for health and fitness? Start working out now.

Live the life now that you want to be living in the future. Your life is never going to magically transform from a stressful, work-filled life to a peaceful, relationship-filled one. You craft your future by the actions and habits you prioritise today.

Live in faith. Live as if that life is already yours. Live a life today that reflects your purpose for tomorrow.

5
Balance

This brings us to the next essential foundation: Relax. Create some balance in your life. Make time for health, fitness, relationships, relaxations and hobbies. Even God took a whole day out to rest.

"On the seventh day God... rested from all his work."
Genesis 2:2 (NLT)

Set your working hours. Have strict "office hours" which allow you time to rest. When you switch off from your business, leave it in the hands of your Father in heaven, He is more than trustworthy.

*"In peace I will lie down and sleep,
for you alone, LORD, make me dwell in safety."*
Psalm 4:8

I know that taking time out isn't always easy with a busy schedule. When I was transitioning from my business as a singing coach into my photography business, I went through a very demanding season. I was effectively running two, full time businesses and was often working 60 or 70 hour a week, which I hated.

I lamented to myself one day, that the thing I miss most about being employed is having set work hours. Once my shift is over I could go home and completely switch off till the next day.

I realised that I was now my own boss so I had the power to set these work hours for myself. So I decided to "employ" myself. I stuck a time sheet up on the fridge and began to "clock" in and out, recording every minute I spent on my business, even the time spent thinking and planning.

My plan was that I would work 40 hours a week and then give myself guilt-free time off. If I worked "overtime", then I would be due time in lieu and I recorded this too.

Within a week I had clocked over 46 hours of lieu time! Oh boy! Even I didn't know how hard I was working. No wonder I was miserable. We are not designed to work all hours, every day of the week. God has set us a very clear example to follow when he took time to rest after his work. If all you ever do is work, you will feel miserable and exhausted and your health and relationships will suffer. Maybe not today, but it will catch up with you and you will experience stress and neglect-related, health and relationship problems.

I began being strict with myself, working within my 40-hour week target and taking the rest of the time to switch off, enjoy old hobbies, go swimming, go to the spa, spend time with friends and spend time in prayer.

I could not believe it but I actually began to fit my work into a 40-hour week! I found unnecessary tasks to cut out and I worked quicker when I was "in the office". My brain was more alert to find creative time-saving solutions. I just seemed to get more done. There seemed to be more hours in the day, and I was so much more satisfied with the work I did.

6
Integrity

*"The one who walks in integrity
will experience a fearless confidence in life..."*
Proverbs 10:9 (TPT)

God blesses honesty, it's as simple as that. When building your own business you will be faced with a myriad of creative ways to compromise your integrity. The challenge with building a God-honouring Business of Blessing is to resist every opportunity for easy, instant gain at the expense of others.

*"Gaining wealth through dishonesty is no gain at all.
But honesty brings you a lasting happiness."*
Proverbs 10:2 (TPT)

Creatively "interpreting" your tax expenses in order to lower your tax bill, for example, may give you more money right now but in the longterm, this is not a recipe for a happy, blessed life. Trust God instead. He knows what you need. Lay your needs before Him and trust Him for the provision to meet it.

*"God won't starve an honest soul,
but he frustrates the appetites of the wicked."*
Proverbs 10:3 (MSG)

God can be trusted to bring you provision and success at the right time, and in the right way, when we look to honour him with honesty and integrity in everything we do. When we take matters into our own hands— bending the truth, twisting the facts or outright deceiving others— we may gain additional momentary riches but we ultimately forfeit the peace to fully enjoy it. We will be restless, discontent and greedy. A life of peace and contentment is worth far more than momentary gain.

7
Excellence

And finally, excellence! Do everything to the best of your ability, as thoroughly and perfectly as you can.

"Put your heart and soul into every activity you do, as though you are doing it for the Lord himself and not merely for others."
Colossians 3:23 (TPT)

Treat every customer as if they are the most valuable customer in the world. Give them your full attention. Work with urgency and dedication and finish with perfection and attention to detail.
When we work as reliably and as passionately as we would if we were working for God Himself, we not only gain peace for ourselves but we also instantly gain one the most valuable and profitable commodities that any business can have: happy customers.

Happy customers will propel your business further than you ever could alone. Happy customers will bring a reach and a reputation, and the connections you could only dream about. Happy customers are the lifeblood of any successful business and this can only be achieved by establishing a commitment to excellence throughout your entire business.

Final Blessing

I hope this has encouraged and inspired you to build and develop your own Business of Blessing. With God in the picture, you have what it takes to build a world-impacting business.

As a final encouragement, take to heart this blessing that God has promised over those who live a life of obedience to His commands. This is the promise over your life and over your business when you walk in obedience, diligence and reckless faith.

"If you fully obey the Lord your God and carefully follow all his commands I give you today, the Lord your God will set you high above all the nations on earth.
All these blessings will come on you and accompany you if you obey the Lord your God:
You will be blessed in the city and blessed in the country.
The fruit of your womb will be blessed, and the crops of your land and the young of your livestock—the calves of your herds and the lambs of your flocks.
Your basket and your kneading trough will be blessed.
You will be blessed when you come in and blessed when you go out.

The Lord will grant that the enemies who rise up against you will be defeated before you. They will come at you from one direction but flee from you in seven.

The Lord will send a blessing on your barns and on everything you put your hand to. The Lord your God will bless you in the land he is giving you.

The Lord will establish you as his holy people, as he promised you on oath, if you keep the commands of the Lord your God and walk in obedience to him.

Then all the peoples on earth will see that you are called by the name of the Lord, and they will fear you.

The Lord will grant you abundant prosperity—in the fruit of your womb, the young of your livestock and the crops of your ground—in the land he swore to your ancestors to give you.

The Lord will open the heavens, the storehouse of his bounty, to send rain on your land in season and to bless all the work of your hands. You will lend to many nations but will borrow from none.

The Lord will make you the head, not the tail. If you pay attention to the commands of the Lord your God that I give you this day and carefully follow them, you will always be at the top, never at the bottom.

Do not turn aside from any of the commands I give you today, to the right or to the left, following other gods and serving them."
Deuteronomy 28:1-14

Keep focused on the prize, set Christ at the heart of everything you do and enjoy the journey!

As I write this, my heart is bursting with excitement for the possibilities that lie ahead of you. I am believing that, for your life and your business, this will be the best year yet!